Calligraphy

AT YOUR FINGERTIPS

Calligraphy

AT YOUR FINGERTIPS

BLITZ EDITIONS

Published by Blitz Editions
an imprint of Bookmart Ltd
Registered Number 2372865
Trading as Bookmart Ltd
Desford Road
Enderby
Leicester LE9 5AD

ISBN: 1 85605 227 3

Material previously published in 1992 as part of the encyclopedia set *Be Creative* (Fabbri Publishing Ltd).

Editorial and design: Brown Packaging Ltd,
255-257 Liverpool Road, London N1 1LX

Printed in the Czech Republic
51743

Contents

SECTION TWO: BOOKMAKING

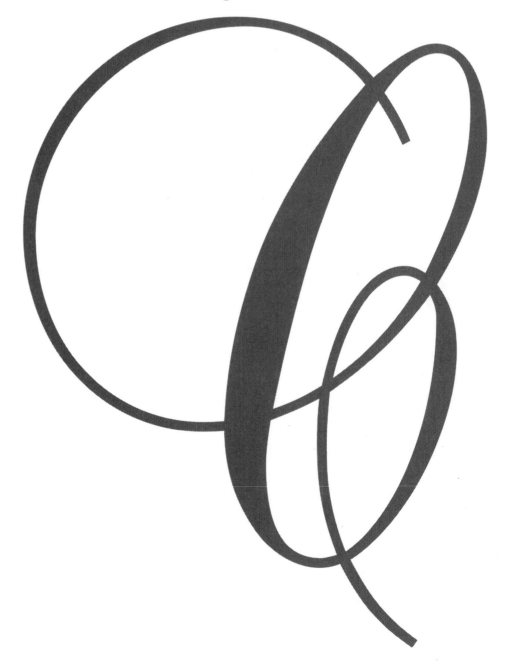

CALLIGRAPHY

An Elegant Hand

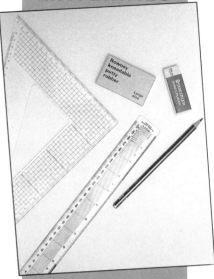

Basic equipment for the calligrapher starts with a set square, ruler, pencil and putty or plastic eraser, *above.*

The craft of calligraphy is as prized today as it has ever been. The services of the professional scribe are in demand for elegantly-lettered invitations, posters, handbills, rolls of honour and family trees. We introduce you to this satisfying craft and show you how to produce your first inscribed lettering in the Foundational Hand.

Above: For paper, start with a layout pad and some cartridge paper. You'll also need a cutting board and cutting tool.

Calligraphy means literally beautiful handwriting, and it is attainable by anyone who can manipulate a pen. It is a craft that can be learned, like any other craft. But when it is used as a means of visually enhancing the written word, it may become an art form. At its most basic level, the practice of calligraphy can be a way to improve one's normal handwriting. At the other extreme, calligraphy can be a means of transforming any written material into something decorative and unique.

Calligraphy has a long history — as long as letterforms themselves. The Foundational Hand used today is based on the incised letterforms used by the ancient Romans to inscribe their monuments. Through the Dark Ages the craft was kept alive in the monasteries by monks producing beautifully illuminated manuscripts, such as *The Book of Kells.*

Today, when the printed word has largely superseded the handwritten word, there is still an enormous demand from commercial art studios and draughtsman's offices for the versatile letterforms that can only be produced by the calligrapher. As the age of the electronically produced letterform advances, so the handwritten

At its most sophisticated level calligraphy can be used to produce decorative designs of scrolls and flourishes, or ornamental display headings, *above.* For ordinary purposes, there is a variety of attractive letterforms available to the practised scribe, some of which are shown *below.*

Foundation

Italic

Uncial

Gothic

Above, calligrapher's ink, cleaning fluid, paintbrush and reservoir, ink eraser, art pen, penholders and various sized nibs.

NAMING THE PARTS

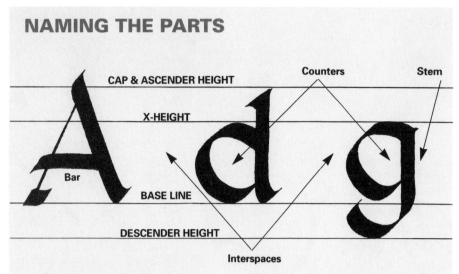

In order to be able to refer to the various parts of a letterform, calligraphers use the terms shown *above*. It is not necessary to memorise these terms at this stage, but this diagram will be a useful reference for future lessons.

letterform becomes more highly prized. The skills of the scribe are in increasing demand.

Any beginner can take up calligraphy and find enjoyment in it. Creating elegant letterforms is soothing and satisfying, and it gives the practitioner the 'feel' of the written word as something unique and valuable. If you are willing to learn and observe the basic rules — and have the determination to practise regularly — you can produce beautiful results.

Equipment

The basic equipment needed for calligraphy are pen, ink and paper. The traditional calligrapher's pen consists of a nib with an ink reservoir, fitted on to a holder. The ink reservoir has to be filled using a paintbrush to transfer the ink from the bottle to reservoir. For the beginner a fountain pen with calligraphic nib is often preferable, because it eliminates the task of constantly refilling. Both types of pen are available with right and left-handed nibs in various sizes.

It is important to use an ink that flows easily and doesn't clog the pen, while giving a good density of colour. Avoid inks which contain drying agents because they can become impossible to remove from a pen even if only left for a short time. If ink residues do become a problem and flushing with water will not shift them, an airbrush cleaning fluid will often remove them.

It gives a better result to work on an angled surface and so a drawing board is another essential piece of equipment. The simplest can be a piece of board that rests on the knee and then leans against a table.

Other items needed are a T-square, if your drawing board has no parallel motion, ruler, set square, HB and 2H pencils, eraser, cutting tool and cutting board. A good light source is essential so if daylight is insufficient, an anglepoise or adjustable table lamp is necessary. You'll also need masking tape, a kitchen roll and a few sheets of cartridge paper.

For preliminary work, use a layout pad. For finished work there are many papers available in a variety of colours. Cartridge paper is good, but usually only available in white, whereas Ingres or cover papers come in many different colours.

First steps

The first thing to do is to practise basic strokes (see *right*). As soon as you move on to letterforms, give some thought to their correct spacing (see *top right*). As you become more experienced, this will become instinctive.

This beautifully illuminated page, *left,* from an English Psalter of the 15th century, depicting the crowning of Henry VI, shows the highly decorative and colourful skills of the medieval scribe.

GETTING STARTED

GUIDELINES

Before starting to make strokes it is necessary to draw up guidelines based on the width of your nib. Using your selected nib, draw a chequerboard pattern as shown *right*, so that the guidelines can then be drawn to give you the correct proportions. The pen is held so that the nib is at right angles to the writing line and the full width of the nib used.

The guidelines will be different for each alphabet used. For the Foundational Hand, which we are using in this lesson, you need to make a chequerboard of 9 nib widths — 3 for ascenders, 4 for x-height and 2 for descenders. The cap height is 6 nib

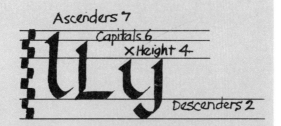

widths. Guidelines can then be projected from the nib widths with a 2H pencil. This procedure is repeated down the sheet (remember to leave a space between the chequerboard groups so that you have a space between the lines of lettering).

HOLDING THE PEN

Hold the pen as shown *left,* resting the nib on the paper at an angle of 30º. The angle of the nib on the paper never changes.

THE NIB

The ink reservoir, *above left,* fits on to the underside of the nib, and has to be filled with ink by dipping a paintbrush in the ink bottle and transferring ink to the reservoir.

LETTER SPACING

HIM

ROO

BEEF

AWAY

To achieve a word that looks evenly spaced, different shaped letters need different spacing. Note that the 0's *above* are set closer together than the straight E's and the oblique letters.

BASIC STROKES

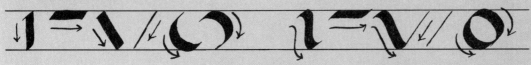

Before starting on lettering proper, it is necessary to practise the basic strokes.

Draw up some pencil guidelines on a sheet of layout paper as shown *left* and, holding your pen with the nib at a 30º angle to the paper (see *above*), practise forming the basic strokes set out on the top line, following the direction of the arrows. Note that the pen almost always moves down or across the paper — not upwards.

Continue to practise these strokes until you can form them cleanly and confidently, before attempting to move on to letterforms.

Before starting to practise the Foundational Hand shown on these pages, set up your drawing board by covering it with two sheets of cartridge paper secured with masking tape. This makes a cushioned surface to write on. Now tape down a sheet of layout paper, rule your guidelines as shown, and you are ready.

Practise the capital letters first, copying the order and direction of strokes shown *top far right*. Remember to keep your nib at a 30° angle, and do not press heavily or you will tear the paper. Keep the model letterforms in front of you where you can see them easily.

When you are fairly confident about the capital letters, you can start on the lower case alphabet. Don't worry if your letters seem clumsy at first — practise makes perfect!

THE FOUNDATIONAL HAND
Completed capital letters

ABCDEFG

HIJKLMN

OPQRSTU

VWXYZ&1

234567890

Completed lower case letters

Ascenders height
7 pen widths
x height
4 pen widths
Descenders
2 pen widths

abcdefghij

klmnopqrstuv

wxyz

STROKES FOR CAPITALS

All the capital letters of the Foundational Hand can be formed using a combination of the basic strokes shown *above*.

Order of strokes for capital letters

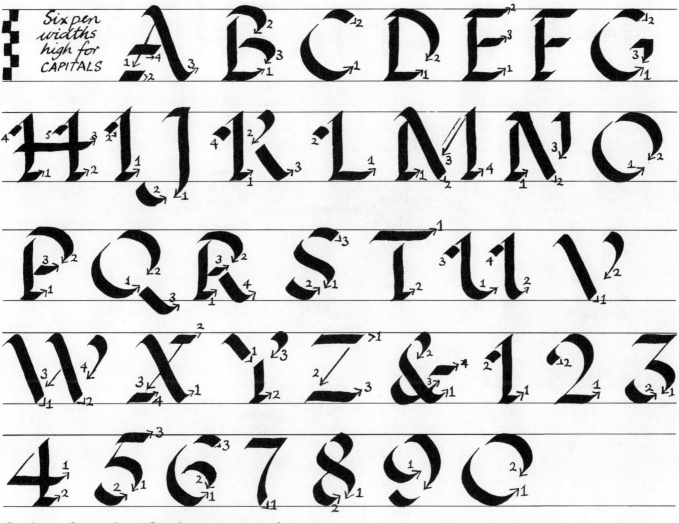

Order of strokes for lower case letters

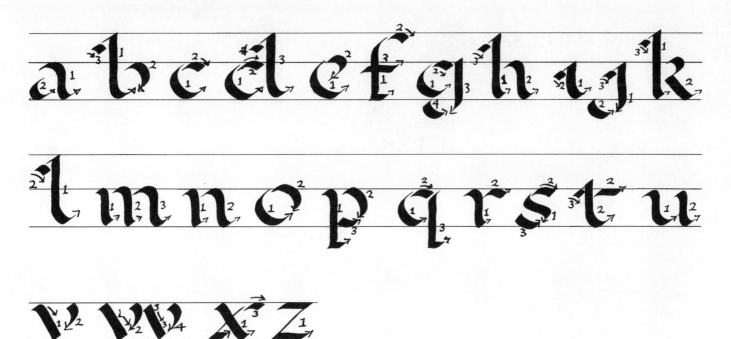

PROJECT

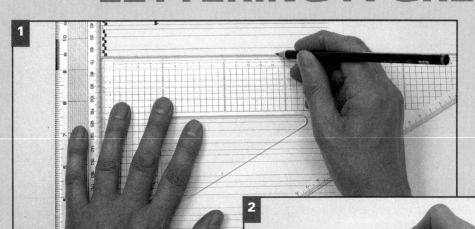

LETTERING A GREETING

1 To try out your new skill, we suggest you letter 'Happy Birthday' for a greeting card. Try it out first on layout paper, as we show here, before doing the final inscription on card. First make the Foundational Hand chequerboard pattern of nib widths, and then rule guidelines for the lettering, using a ruler and set square.

2 Lay a sheet of blotting paper over the lower half of your layout paper to protect it (paper that has picked up oil from the hands will not accept ink). Now you are ready to make the first downward stroke of the H.

3 Carry on lettering, following the order of strokes set out on page 4. Remember to try and space the letters correctly, so that they are neither too close together, nor too far apart. This is something that gets easier with practice.

4 When you have completed lettering 'Happy Birthday' look at it critically. Have you followed the sequence of strokes shown, and did you keep the nib always at the same angle? Could you improve on the letter spacing? When you are satisfied, you are ready to copy it on to a plain card. Keep all your old work — you can learn a lot from past mistakes!

CALLIGRAPHY

The italic hand

MATERIALS

For the invitation shown *below left* you will need:

Above, drawing board; T-square; ruler; set square; pencil; A3 layout pad; masking tape.

Above, black felt-tip pen; eraser; pen holder; nibs (2, 3, 3^1/$_2$ Mitchell/Rexel) and reservoirs; non-waterproof black ink; scissors; paper paste; envelopes; tissue; piece of paper to protect your work.

In our first calligraphy lesson we introduced you to the basic techniques of the craft and demonstrated the Foundational Hand. In this lesson we concentrate on the Italic Hand and show you how to put your new 'hand' to practical use in our step-by-step lettering of an invitation.

Menus, invitations, posters and all manner of calligraphic work can be enlivened by the rhythmic flow of the Italic Hand. It is characterised by a slight forward slope, a compressed form (being based on an oval 'o' rather than the circular 'o' of the Foundational Hand) and the sweeping strokes used to make the arches of letters such as 'a' and 'n', all of which contribute to making this a hand that can, with practice, be written at some speed.

You should first practise the letters of the lower case and capital alphabet using a medium-sized nib (here a size 2 Mitchell/Rexel nib), following the guidelines given. It is best to practise the letters in groups of similar forms that relate to one another, rather than going through the letters in alphabetical order. To make the upward sweeping strokes of the 'a' and other letters in this group, you will have to push against the edge of the nib, something that is generally to be avoided with other scripts. Remember, as always, that the shape of the space inside the letters is just as important as the strokes themselves.

Once you have mastered the lower case and capital letters, work on getting letter and word spacing even, using the same nib before you try using a smaller nib or changing the x-height of the letters.

The paste-up process described for the invitation project is a useful way of designing a piece of work both for an original one-off piece, or in preparation for printing. Before you begin on the project, decide on the wording and size of your invitation, and check that you can get envelopes to fit. Photocopying is a cheaper alternative to printing when producing small quantities, so talk to your local printer and make sure that the paper or card they have available is suitable, and that their photocopying machine will produce good quality copies. The invitation is designed to be copied on to A4 paper (standard typing paper size) and folded so that it will stand up. You can copy on to coloured paper or card, and some machines will copy in colour.

Above: A detail from a manuscript written by Francesco Moro in Italy in the second half of the 16th century that makes exhuberant use of flourishing to embellish the italic hand.

ITALIC GUIDELINES

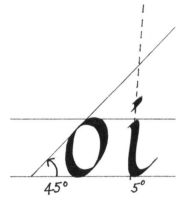

Above: The x-height of the lower case letters is 5 nib widths high, the ascenders and descenders are an additional 4 nib widths; the capitals are 7 nib widths high.

Above: The angle of the pen nib to the writing line is 45° for nearly all the strokes, with some exceptions. The writing slopes slightly to the right — about 5-10°.

Above: With italic you will have to break the rule of not pushing the pen because some of the strokes sweep upwards in an anticlockwise direction (as in a, d, g, q, u, y) and in a clockwise direction (as in n, b, h, k, m, r).

THE ITALIC HAND
Lower case letters

abcdefghij

klmnopqrs

tuvwxyyz

1234567890

Order of strokes for lower case letters

Capital letters

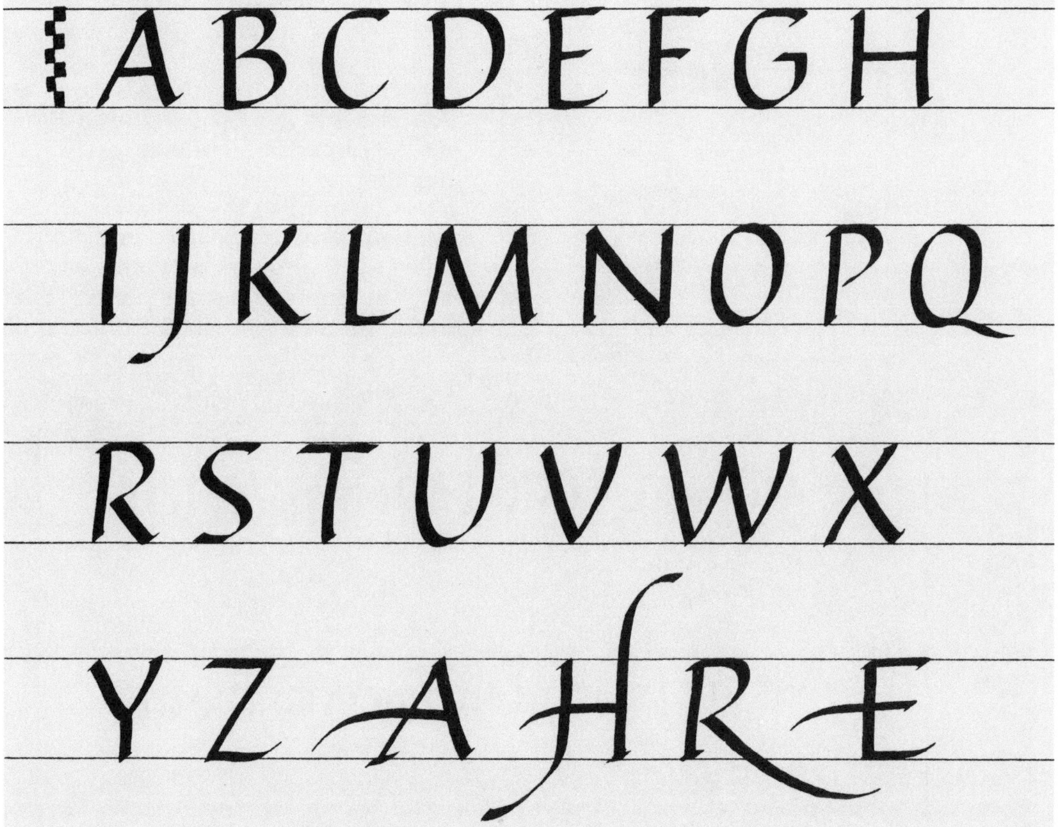

ABCDEFGH
IJKLMNOPQ
RSTUVWX
YZAHRE

Order of strokes for capital letters

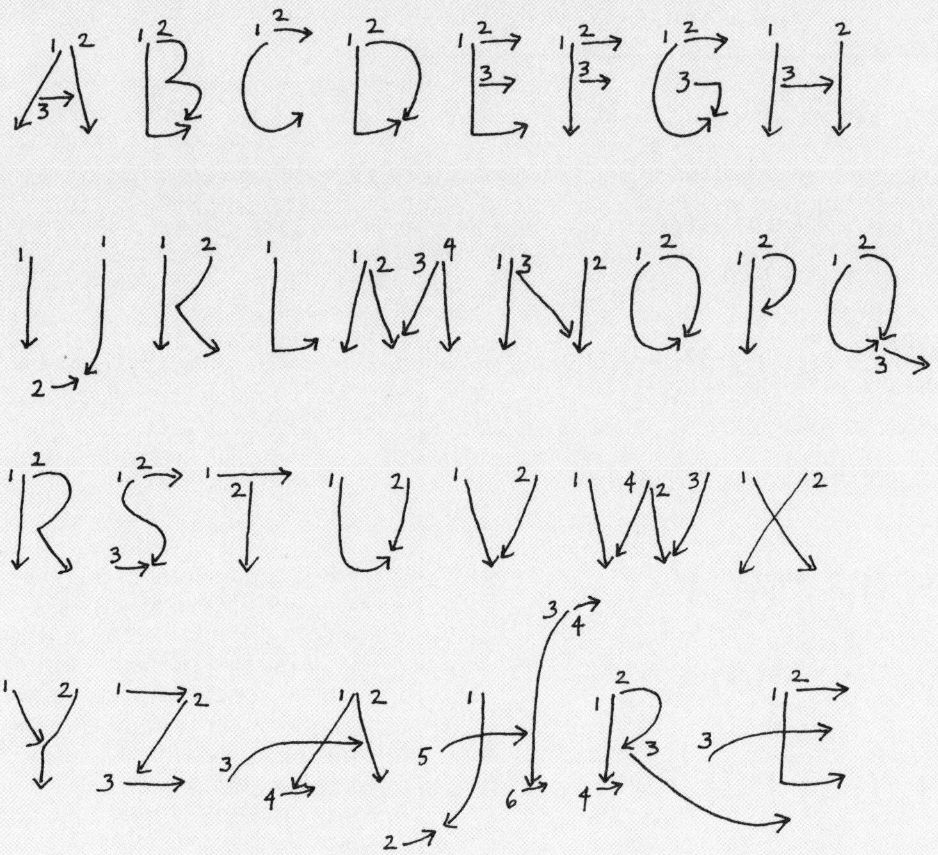

ABCDEFGH
IJKLMNOPQ
RSTUVWX
YZAHRE

Changing the pen angle

ZX
ZX
NN

Above: In order to avoid too great a contrast between the thickness of some of the diagonal strokes, you will have to change the angle of the nib. To thicken the second stroke of the X and the diagonal of Z, turn the nib to a shallower angle. To make the two vertical strokes of N thinner steepen the angle of the nib a little.

Changing the x-height

nn

Above: To vary the weight of the letter, change the x-height. Here a lower case 'n' is written at a height of 5 and 4 nib widths. The project uses lower case letters at an x-height of 4 nib widths.

PROJECT

LETTERING THE INVITATION

*Angela and Robert
invite you to a
housewarming party
at 41 Cleveland Avenue, Manchester
on Friday 9th December at 7·30*

1 Cover the board with a sheet of paper as in Calligraphy Lesson 1. Using masking tape, stick a sheet of layout paper over the paper on the board, aligning the edge with a T-square. Using a T-square and a set square, map out the dimensions of the invitation in pencil (A4 is 210 x 297mm, so the invitation will be folded to make a card 210 x 148.5mm), and in your own handwriting plan out the general arrangement of the lines.

2 In order to select a suitable nib size, write out the longest line with nibs of different sizes at an x-height of 5 nib widths to see which works best. Nib size 2 is too large, size 3 is nearly right. Rather than using a smaller nib, change the x-height to 4 nib widths to make a shorter line (remember that you need to allow for generous margins around the writing).

at 41 Cleveland Avenue
size 2 nib
(at 5 nib-widths x height)

at 41 Cleveland Avenue, Manchester
size 3 nib
(at 5 nib-widths x height)

at 41 Cleveland Avenue, Manchester
size 3 nib
(at 4 nib-widths x height)

*Angela and Robert   invite you to a
housewarming party
at 41 Cleveland Avenue, Manchester
on Friday 9th December at 7·30*

*Angela and Robert   Angela   Angela
at   AT   on   ON   R·S·V·P   R S V P
invite you to a   on Friday 9th December at 7·30*

housewarming party

Housewarming party

Housewarming party

3 Rule up a sheet of paper for writing with a size 3 nib at an x-height of 4 nib widths and write out all the text of the invitation. Rewrite words that you are not happy with, or wish to change. To emphasise the words 'Housewarming party', use a wider nib (size 2, at an x-height of 4 nib widths); the RSVP is written with a size 3½ nib.

4 Using a T-square and a set square, map out the dimensions of the invitation in pencil on another sheet of paper and draw a central vertical and horizontal line. Using scissors, cut out the lines of lettering you have written for the invitation and arrange them by eye. To centre the lines, fold them in half and stick in place with dabs of paste, matching the fold with the central vertical line.

5 Stick all the lines in place, considering alternatives to your original idea. Draw the border with a 3½ nib.

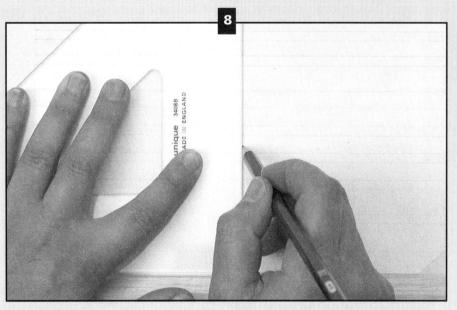

6 On a strip of paper, mark off the baseline and top of the x-heights of all the lines.

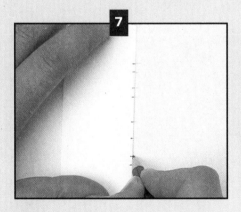

7 Standardise any line spaces that you want to be the same (ie between lines 1 and 2 and 4, 5 and 6, which have a baseline to baseline space of 3 x-heights). If necessary, adjust the measurements on your original strip of paper and mark out a new strip. Transfer these measurements on to a fresh piece of layout paper, marked out to the format of the invitation.

8 Rule the writing lines, then draw a vertical line in the centre with the set square.

9 Remove the strips of lettering from the paste-up and place them on the paper that protects your work. Use them as a guide to check that the spacing is consistent as you start to write out the finished invitation.

10 Write out all the text and then draw the borders. These are simple zig-zags drawn at an angle of approximately 45°. When the zig-zags are dry, put in the dots (see below). When you have finished working, wipe the nibs and reservoirs clean with a piece of tissue.

invite you to a

Housewarming party

at

41 Cleveland Avenue, Manchester

on Friday 9th December at 7·30

· R · S · V · P ·

11 When the ink is dry, cut the paper to size and rub out the pencil lines. Take the invitation to a printer to copy on to coloured paper or thin card. The printer will fold the invitation for you, or you can do this yourself.

The envelopes can be written in your own handwriting, or in italics. Try writing without any guidelines, or just with a baseline. You could use a coloured felt-tip pen to match the colour of the invitation.

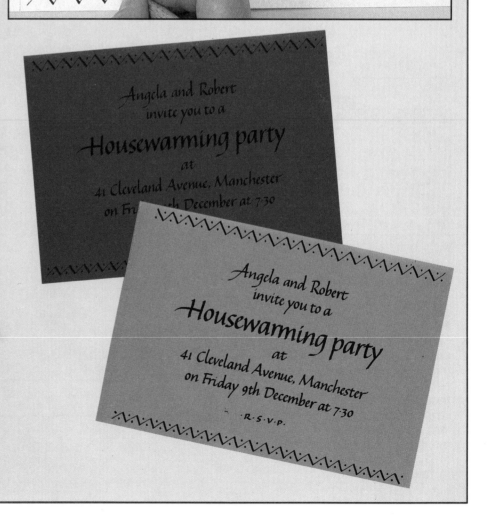

CALLIGRAPHY

The Gothic Hand

MATERIALS

For the quotation shown *below left* you will need:

Above, drawing board; masking tape; non-waterproof black ink; plastic rule; pair of dividers (for ruling lines); layout pad; pen holder; No 1 Mitchell/Rexel nib; pencil; black fibre tip pen with fine nib.

Above, palette; tube of spectrum red designers gouache; sheet of A3 Ingres paper; steel rule; rag; scissors; watercolour brush, size 1 or 2; eraser; cow gum; scalpel; bulldog clip.

Our third calligraphy lesson introduces you to the Gothic hand, a classic script that has always had popular appeal because of its distinctive appearance and the way it combines so well with decoration.

The Gothic script is probably the most familiar of all the historic calligraphic hands. In varying forms it was in use all over Europe from the 12th to the 15th centuries. It can be seen, for example, in the Books of Hours, which were designed for the nobility, and in many manuscripts created outside the monasteries to fill the demand for knowledge of an ever-widening section of the population. This increase in learning led to an enormous growth in the production of books. Many of these have survived and are in museums and libraries all over the world.

The overriding characteristic of these books is their use of black lettering, illuminated by richly coloured and gilded decoration (see page 21). In a later lesson we will show you how to create these illuminated letters. In this lesson we are concentrating on the Gothic script itself.

The Gothic script has three main elements which, taken together, give it its distinctive textured appearance. First, the letters are tall and narrow and written close together. This upright form echoes the Gothic church architecture of the medieval period, with its pointed arches and flying buttresses. Second, the letters usually appear heavy and very black when compared with other hands, which is why Gothic is sometimes called Black Letter. Third, the letters are sharply angular, most of them having very few curved lines. Today, the Gothic script is generally used for decorative purposes rather than for conveying information.

Easy to learn

In spite of its ornate appearance, the Gothic hand is one of the easiest to learn as it is composed of a few basic shapes. As you begin to write, forget the familiar shapes of ordinary letters and concentrate on the basic shapes of the Gothic script. These are combined in different ways to form the individual letters of the alphabet. The words are formed by packing the letters together — they should more or less touch at the top and bottom — and the words themselves also stand close together, giving Gothic its dense and textured appearance.

LOWER CASE BASIC STROKES

The diamond shape, **1**, and the vertical stroke, **2**, form the basis of most letters. When combining them, as in **3** and **4**, begin by using three separate strokes. As you become more experienced you will be able to combine them in a single stroke.

Take care to maintain the pen angle at 45° in strokes **6** and **7**.

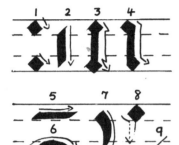

PEN ANGLE

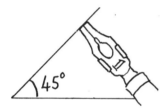

Hold pen at 45° for all strokes except stroke 5, which is shallower (35° approximately).

Stroke 8 occurs in c and r and helps to fill an otherwise large space. After making the wedge shape turn the pen on to the lower corner and pull down.

Stroke 9 Hairline (very thin) strokes are made by moving the nib along its width in either direction.

Completed lower case letters

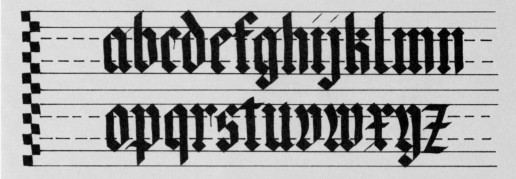

Order of strokes for lower case letters

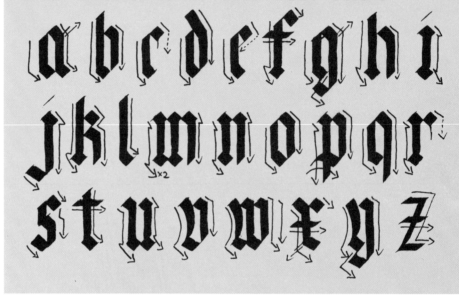

GUIDE LINES

Rule up your page using the chequerboard *below*, made with a No 1 Mitchell/Rexel nib.

With the nib at 45°, draw two diamonds at the top and bottom of the x-height, as shown *below*. Rule in the extra lines.

The guide sheet

A guide sheet can be used when you are practising your lettering, and this means you do not have to rule up every page separately.

Rule up one sheet with dark lines using a drawing pen or fine fibre tip. When this is placed under layout paper it will show through. Fix the guide sheet and layout paper together with masking tape so that they cannot slip

Ruling up with dividers

.The most accurate way to rule up a guide sheet for practising or an actual project is to use a pair of dividers. Make the chequerboard as shown *left*, and rule up the first set of lines and the top line of the second set. Here the bottom line of one set is the top line of the second set, but this will not always be the case.

Now take your dividers and set them with one point on the top line of the first set and the other on the top line of the second set. Then 'walk' them down the edge of the page for as many lines as you require. Without altering the width of the dividers, repeat the process from each of the lines you have ruled. Unless you are ruling up with a T-square, repeat the process on the opposite edge of the sheet and then rule up.

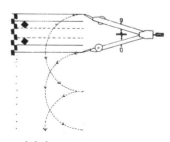

It is important to use dividers that have a screw to fix the position and to be as accurate as possible when you rule between the pin-points.

Completed capital letters

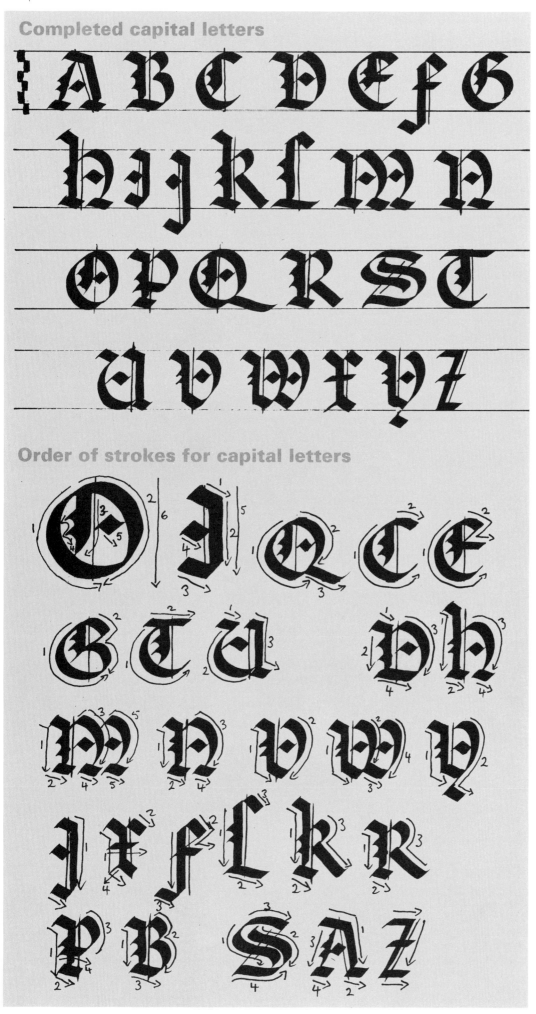

Order of strokes for capital letters

BASIC STROKES FOR CAPITAL LETTERS

Practise the basic strokes first, and then practise the letters in groups of similar forms as set out on the lower half of this page.

The decorative strokes are added at the end. If you find the vertical hairlines difficult you can use a fine, pointed nib.

Basic strokes

Decorative strokes

CAPITAL LETTERS

The capital letters are 5½ nib widths high, making them just a little shorter than the ascenders of lower case letters. They stand out because they are mainly curved, in contrast to the vertical emphasis of the lower case letters.

The Gothic script was used extensively in the highly decorated manuscripts of the Middle Ages, such as the St Omar Psalter (c.1330), *above*.

PROJECT

LETTERING AND DECORATING A QUOTATION

1 Choose a quotation that appeals to you and write it out in the Gothic script on layout paper, using your guide sheet. Our quotation is written with the nib size you have been practising with, a No 1 Mitchell/Rexel.

2 Cut your writing into strips or separate words and arrange them to form an attractive block of lettering. Stick the pieces down on to another sheet of layout paper. Use cow gum so that you can peel the words off and move them if necessary. Avoid large gaps between the words and between lines. Remember that this script looks best when it forms a close-knit texture. Leave enough space around the capital to allow for decoration.

3 If you wish to add the attribution (the name of the author) do it at this stage. Very small, spaced out Foundational capitals are used here (see pages 10-11). If you do not feel comfortable using a very small nib, you could use a black fibre-tip pen with a fine nib.

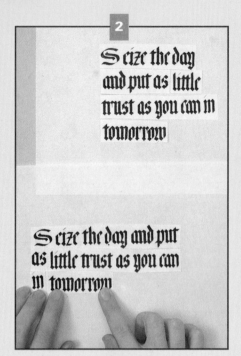

4 When you are happy with the layout, rewrite the text on a fresh piece of layout paper. Make two or three photocopies so that you can try out various forms of decoration. Choose paper for the finished work that will go well with the frame. We have used a coloured Ingres paper, but you can use smooth watercolour paper.

5 The most suitable medium for the decoration is gouache. Squeeze a little colour on to a palette and dilute with water until it is the consistency of thin cream. For the best results, use a fine, good-quality watercolour brush. Draw the decoration lightly with pencil and then colour it in, painting carefully around the initial letter. It has to be done this way as the ink will spread if you try to write on top of gouache. The fine black lines of the decoration — and this can include the hairlines on the initial — are added with a fine fibre tip at the end.

6 Rule up your piece of paper for your completed work. Place your rough where you can see it clearly and make your final copy, including the decoration. Leave a little more space at the bottom than the top. The side margins should be approximately the same width as the top. Use a sheet of paper larger than the frame and trim it down after you have done the lettering.

The Gothic hand lends itself particularly well to classic literary quotations such as those from Shakespeare and the Bible.

CALLIGRAPHY

The Uncial hand

The Uncial script is one of the most beautiful alphabets in the history of lettering. Its clear, simple shapes are easy to read and provide a strong contrast to the Gothic hand you learned in our previous calligraphy lesson. Here we show you how to combine Uncials with watercolour pencils to make an attractive thankyou card.

The Uncial alphabet developed during the 4th century as the Roman Empire was beginning to crumble away. Like the Roman alphabet it consists only of capital letters. Because it is essentially a book hand (it was not used for inscriptions on stone but only for manuscripts) we can see how the scribe's need for speed is beginning to alter the form of the letters — some of the letters have ascenders and descenders, to avoid confusing them, and others such as 'A' have acquired a form that was easy to write.

The Uncial script that you will learn in this lesson is based on a tiny book that was found buried in the tomb of St Cuthbert, who died in AD 687. It is the Gospel of John in Latin, known as the Stonyhurst Gospel, and it can be seen in the British Museum.

The main characteristics of the hand are: first, a pen angle of approximately 15°, which is much flatter than in previous hands we have studied; and second, a low x-height of $3^{1}/_{2}$ nib widths. These two factors together produce wide, rounded letters with a wide white space within them. You will need to practise to get used to this flatter angle — you should also concentrate on making the space between the letters match the space inside them.

This lesson involves the use of a double pencil. By using this tool, which is simple to make, you can see very clearly whether your 'pen' angle is consistent, so that the thick or thin parts of the letters occur in the right place, and whether the strokes join each other correctly. An added bonus is that you can rub the letters out if you do not get them right the first time.

Once you have mastered the technique, a double pencil can be used to practise any alphabet — this will give you a whole new range of possibilities for developing your calligraphic skills.

MATERIALS

For the card shown *below left* you will need:

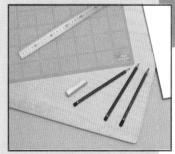

Above, drawing board; layout paper; two HB pencils; one 2H pencil; eraser; steel ruler; cutting board.

Above, good quality white paper and envelope (see helpful hint, *below*); non-waterproof black ink; pen holder and reservoir; Mitchell/Rexel nibs 1, $1^{1}/_{2}$ and 2; watercolour pencils; waterproof fibre-tip pen, fine; good quality size 2 watercolour brush; cow gum; masking tape; scalpel.

HELPFUL HINT

Envelopes come in a limited range of sizes. Our card is designed to fit one measuring 110 x 220mm. For this you will need a sheet of paper at least 220 x 220mm, but you may wish to buy larger or smaller sheets, in which case you will have to make sure that you buy suitable envelopes.

GUIDE LINES

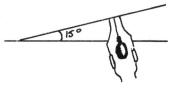

The x-height is 3½ nib widths, ascenders and descenders 5 nib widths. The space between the x-height on the line above and the line below is approximately 1½ times the x-height.

PEN ANGLE

The pen angle is 15°. You will need to practise this, as it is a much flatter angle than that used for previous alphabets.

THE UNCIAL HAND

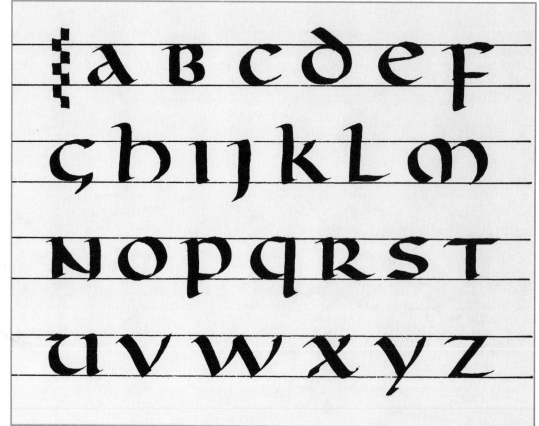

LETTERS ARRANGED IN FAMILY GROUPS

The counters of O, C, D, E and G are similar. The start of the second stroke in O and similar letters should overlap the first stroke.

The same shaped counter appears in part in Q, U, M, P and H.

The curve at the top of B and R is more rounded than in F and S.

The diagonal stroke of Z is made with the pen held in a horizontal position to avoid a weak, skinny letter.

The wide diagonal strokes from left to right are made with a steeper pen angle, approximately 30°.

THE UNCIAL HAND WRITTEN WITH A DOUBLE PENCIL

MAKING AND USING A DOUBLE PENCIL

1 Using a craft knife or scalpel, cut a flat side on two HB pencils.

2 Fix the pencils firmly together with masking tape.

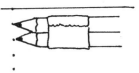

3 Calculate the x-height; the space between the pencil points is the 'nib width'.

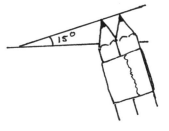

4 Practise holding the pencils at a 15° angle.

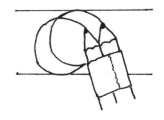

5 Writing like this will come with practice. Try to maintain equal pressure on both points.

PROJECT

A THANKYOU CARD

1 Using a double pencil, write the word 'thankyou' on a piece of layout paper, positioning the word so that there is a fairly wide margin all around it. The amount of space the word takes up will be the determining factor in the size of the finished card.

4 Using the lettering as a guide, calculate the size your card should be and rule up on good quality paper accordingly. If you can, allow a little more than you need for the side margins so that you can trim them to centre your work if necessary. A good method for ruling up this type of card is given in the lesson on the Italic hand. Follow steps 6-8 on page 17, making any necessary adaptations for the thankyou card.

7 Colour in the letters and then go over them with the paintbrush dipped in water. When dry, trim the card and fold it.

2 Using layout paper, write out the word in double pencil several times. Go over the pencil lines with a fine black waterproof fibre-tip or drawing pen (if you use calligraphic ink it will run when you add the colour). Try out various colour schemes using watercolour pencils.

5 Write out the pen lettering first (you can make adjustments to the pencil work but not to the ink).

6 Make sure the ink is dry, then write in the pencilled word. If any letter looks badly written you can rub it out and try again. When

3 On another sheet of layout paper write out the rest of the message several times using various nib sizes — for example, 1 $1\frac{1}{2}$ or 2. Cut these into separate strips and combine them with the double pencil work to see which gives the most attractive and balanced effect. There is no hard and fast rule about the amount of space between the lines; use your eye to decide this. For our card we used a No $1\frac{1}{2}$ nib.

you are satisfied, go over the pencil lines with the fibre-tip or drawing pen (see step 2). Rub out all the pencil lines.

CALLIGRAPHY

VERSALS

MATERIALS

To make the change of address card shown *below left* you will need:

Above, drawing board; layout paper; one piece of Saunders Waterford 90lb HP paper, 210 x 210mm, folded in half; plastic ruler; eraser; pencil; scissors; prit stick.

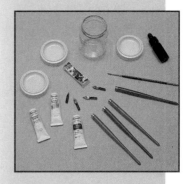

Above, three Mitchell/Rexel nibs with reservoirs, Nos 3$\frac{1}{2}$, 4 and 5; one pointed nib; penholders; designers gouache in cerulean blue, cool grey No 2 and red ochre; dropper and bottle; jar; three small dishes, or palette, for mixing colours; small artist's brush; chopstick rest (optional) for holding pens and brushes.

In this calligraphy lesson we show you how to build up Versals with harmonious letter shapes based on Roman capitals. We have combined these elegant letters with the Italic hand to make a colourful change of address card.

The term 'Versals' was given to capital letters built up with several strokes of the pen, which were often used at the beginning of verses or chapters of text in medieval manuscripts. The underlying structure of classical Versal letters is based on the skeleton form of the Roman alphabet, so it is useful to have a good understanding of these forms first.

Practise the Roman skeleton letters on the next page in their related family groups as they are shown. They have been arranged in groups that relate in terms of proportions; the explanation of their geometric construction will help you to see this more clearly. When you have mastered the basic shapes of these letters, you can go on to build up the Versal letters.

The Versals exemplar is written with a Mitchell/Rexel No 4 nib at an x-height of 24 nib-widths, while the Versals in the project are written with a No 5 nib at an x-height of 18 nib-widths, which makes them a heavier weight, even though a thinner nib is used. You will find that changing the weight of letters also affects proportions and spacing.

We have used designers gouache for the writing and the illustration. Each colour is mixed with water in a shallow container. The consistency at which paint will flow in a nib is similar to that of single cream. Add the water to the gouache, a little at a time. This is easily done using a dropper, which can be bought from a chemists. Load the pen with paint, using a brush. The paint needs to be brushed generously down between the reservoir and the nib on the underside of the nib, as illustrated *right*.

SKELETON CAPITALS

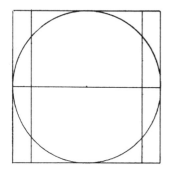

A circle inside a square is the framework on which all the letters are based. 'Circular' letters occupy the full circle; 'rectangular' letters occupy a rectangle that is three-quarters the width of the square and is slightly less than the area of the circle; 'narrow' letters are based on half the width of the square.

SPACING

To achieve evenly-spaced words with these skeleton letters you will have to space them widely. Start with a letter space of $5/8$ the height of the letter between two straight-sided letters. The space between all other letter shapes should appear to be the same as this. So, for example, a straight-sided letter can be a little closer to a curved letter, and two curved letters can be closer still.

PEN-WRITTEN SKELETON CAPITALS

The skeleton Roman capitals *right* have been written with a No 4 nib at an x-height of 125mm. Notice that the forms are slightly modified to create more pleasing shapes; for example, the bowl of P and R is larger than the geometric form, and W is slightly narrower than two Vs.

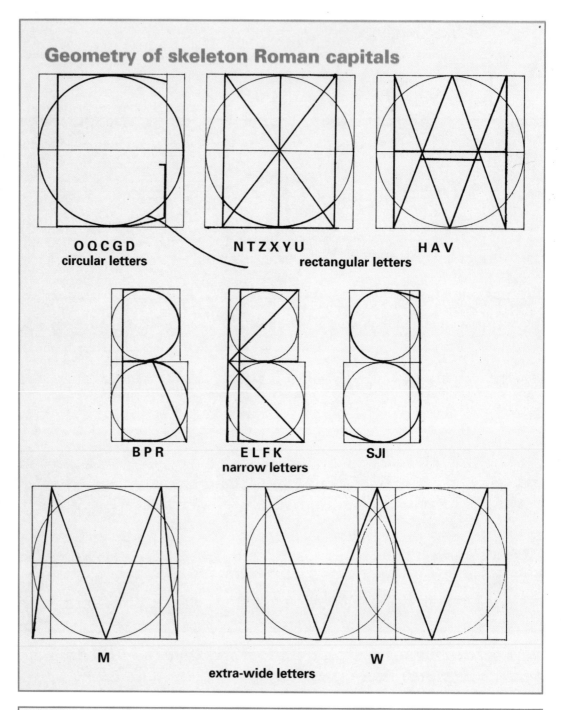

Geometry of skeleton Roman capitals

O Q C G D
circular letters

N T Z X Y U
rectangular letters

H A V

B P R

E L F K
narrow letters

S J I

M

W

extra-wide letters

Skeleton Roman capitals grouped by proportion

A H N T U V X Y Z
Rectangular letters

E F L B P R K S J I
Narrow letters

C G D O O Q   M W
Circular letters   Extra-wide letters

Versals grouped by proportion

AHNTUV
Rectangular letters

XYZ IEFLB

PRKSJMW

CGDOQ
Circular letters

Construction of Versals

AHNTUV

XYZ IEFLB

PRKSJMW

CGDOQ

BASIC FORM OF VERSALS

The basic form of Versals is based on skeleton Roman capitals. The O is circular with an oval inside shape.

WEIGHT

Write the letters with a No 4 nib at a height that is 8 times the stem width. As the stem width is 3 nib-widths this means the height is 24 nib-widths. Remember that you can alter the weight of the letters by changing the letter height or by changing the nib size.

PEN ANGLE

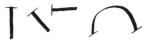

The pen is turned to give its broadest stroke for stems, arms and diagonals, and to give its thinnest stroke for serifs. Curves are made with the nib held at a slight angle.

CONSTRUCTION

The diagram (*left*) shows the construction and order of strokes for the letters. A final stroke fills in the stems, so the thick straight lines, curves and diagonals are actually made up of 3 strokes. Thin strokes (for example the verticals of N) are one main stroke with weight subtly added.

PROJECT

CHANGE OF ADDRESS CARD

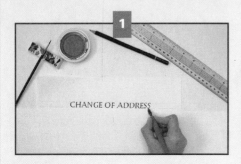

1 With a pencil, rule up for the Versals on a piece of layout paper, at an x-height of 18 nib-widths, using a No 5 nib. Mix up the cerulean blue paint in a palette, adding enough water to allow the paint to flow through the nib. Apply some colour to the nib (see page 27) and write the words 'Change of address' in Versals.

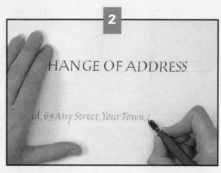

2 Again using layout paper, rule up for the address, which is written in Italic with a No 3½ nib at an x-height of 5 nib-widths. Mix up some cool grey No 2 and write out your new address in a continuous line (ready to cut out later for the paste-up).

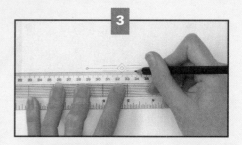

3 On layout paper, practise the decorative design that will go at the top of your card. To draw the design, use a ruler to draw a horizontal line in pencil and in the centre measure out the larger diamond, which is 10mm from corner to corner. For the grey central line, measure 30mm from either side of the diamond and pencil in the arrow heads at each end. Draw the narrow blue lines on the design (15mm in length and 20mm away from the horizontal central line) and draw in the second diamond shape in the centre of the first one.

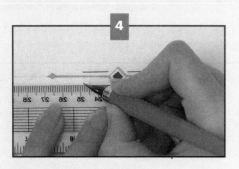

4 Mix up some red ochre paint and paint the diamond. Use a 3½ nib for the thick lines in grey and a pointed nib for the thin lines (the pointed nib does not have a reservoir).

5 Still using layout paper, draw a rectangle 210 x 105mm, which are the dimensions of the completed, folded card. Draw a central vertical line. Cut out your

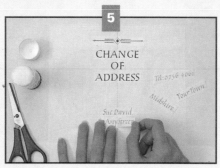

lines of text and the decorative design and centre them across the vertical central line. To centre the lines of text, fold them in half. Position them carefully to allow even spacing between the lines of Versals and between the lines of Italic. Allow enough space between the text for the drawing of the castle. Using prit stick, paste the text and design in their correct positions.

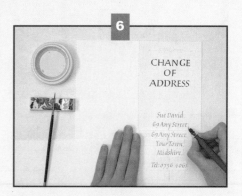

6 Using a pencil, rule up lightly on your piece of card, following your rough layout. Draw a central vertical line again as you did in Step 5. With a pencil, mark out the length of each writing line. Write out the words, using your rough to check the spacing. Fold under each completed layout line as you go along. Pencil in the decorative design and draw it with the 3½ nib and the pointed nib.

7 Pencil in the castle design and go over the lines with paint using the pointed nib. When dry, rub out the pencil lines.

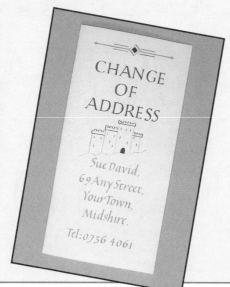

If you wish, you can substitute a design of your own for the castle or choose a different colour scheme for your card. The completed card will fit in a standard envelope measuring 218 x 108mm.

CALLIGRAPHY

COLOUR AND CALLIGRAPHY

Mary, Mary,
quite contrary,
how does your garden grow?
with silver bells
and cockle shells,
and pretty maids
all in a row.

MATERIALS

To produce the nursery rhyme shown *below left* you will need:

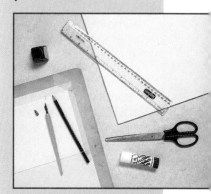

Above, drawing board; A3 layout paper; scissors; ruler; prit stick; H pencil; non-waterproof black ink; pen holder; Mitchell/Rexel 2¹/₂ nib and reservoir.

Above, watercolours (pan or tubes); palette; designer's gouache in cadmium yellow pale, cerulean blue, alizarin crimson, white, ultramarine and silver; gum sandarac; clarified ox gall; artist's brushes, sizes 1 and 6; two small inexpensive brushes.

In this lesson we take a detailed look at the use of colour in calligraphy, and show you how to letter a subtly-coloured rhyme.

Now that you are improving your lettering skills, colour can be used to add a new dimension to your work. In practical terms, colour can be used to pick out or emphasise a particular word or line. It can also be used emotively, to express your own subjective response to a text.

In this lesson we will look at different ways of using colour, some quite bold, others more restrained. Colour can be introduced in the background, either by using a coloured paper or by creating a coloured background yourself. Or you can use colour in the pen to create coloured lettering. You may want to write the text in one colour throughout, or change the colour line by line, or randomly.

In the following pages we discuss the advantages and disadvantages of using gouache, watercolours and coloured inks, as well as providing you with guidelines on how to use them.

HELPFUL HINT

Calligrapher's materials, including a range of papers in a variety of colours, can be obtained from most good art shops. If you want to use fibre tip calligraphy pens, buy paper specially made for use with marker pens to give a sharper edge to your strokes.

BASIC PRINCIPLES

GOUACHE

The paint most often used by calligraphers is designer's gouache, which produces an opaque finish. It can also be thinned with water for a more transparent effect. You do not need to purchase an array of colours; if you choose a few basic ones you can use them to mix others. Some colours, such as most browns and viridian, do not flow very well from the pen and are therefore better mixed from the range suggested *below*.

If you mix your own colours you will often get a better result and obtain subtler colours than the commercially-produced ones.

BASIC COLOURS

The colours listed below are those we suggest for use with calligraphy. When purchasing gouache, check the labels for colour permanency, which is either indicated in letters or with a star.

Cadmium red, alizarin crimson, ultramarine, oxide of chromium, cadmium yellow, lemon yellow, cerulean blue, lamp black, zinc white or permanent white

You may also wish to buy gold and silver gouache. These produce good results if they are mixed to the right consistency. They are unsuitable for work of a more permanent nature as the colour will eventually blacken. They are, however, useful for short-lived greetings cards.

USEFUL MATERIALS

In addition to the project materials needed for this lesson, there are some other basic materials, shown below, that you will need. It is not necessary to purchase all of them at one time — you can build up a collection gradually — and you will probably find that you already have several of them, particularly if you have done other projects.

Above, **a selection of coloured papers, smooth and textured (see opposite page); fixative; watercolours (tubes or pan); coloured inks; mortar and pestle (for grinding gum sandarac); coloured pencils; pastels; automatic pen; masking fluid.**

MIXING COLOURS

To mix gouache for writing, squeeze out a small amount on to a saucer or palette and gradually add drops of clean water from a brush. Mix until the paint becomes the consistency of thin cream. Make sure that you mix the paint thoroughly so that no lumps remain.

If you want to mix two or more than two colours together, start with the lighter colour and gradually add the darker one. It is best to have different brushes for the various colours. Brushes for paint mixing need not be expensive ones.

When lettering a large piece of work, make certain you mix enough colour to finish the work. Even if you keep notes on the colours you used and the proportions, matching the colour at a later date is very difficult. Mixed gouache can be stored in glass jars; miniature jam jars are ideal for this purpose.

Once you have mixed your colour, brush a little of it on to the nib, making certain that the paint has gone inside the reservoir (see page 27). While you are writing, stir the paint in the palette often to prevent the colours separating, and clean the nib occasionally to prevent the paint drying on it.

If you have difficulty in getting the gouache to write, check that your reservoir is not too tight on the nib and that the gouache is not too thick. A few drops of ox gall (available from art shops) added to the paint will help the flow in the pen.

BASIC PRINCIPLES

WATERCOLOUR AND INKS

For a more translucent colour use artist's quality watercolour paints. These are available in tubes or pans. The pans contain better quality colours, but the tubes are more convenient to use, especially if you are mixing larger quantities of colour. It is especially important to ensure that clean brushes and water are used when mixing watercolours, as translucency will be lost if the water is murky.

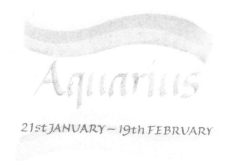

21st JANUARY – 19th FEBRUARY

'*Aquarius*' written in watercolour, with the dates in gouache

COLOURED BACKGROUNDS

Now that you know how to mix your colours, try using them with a pen. Write a text in gouache with one colour on white paper to see if you have the consistency that keeps your writing sharp. Then try the same colour on a darker paper. Not all colours are effective on dark paper and if the colour is mixed too thinly it will merge into the background. With the exception of bright reds and yellows, most colours will need to have white mixed with them.

Good coloured papers for writing on are available from most art shops. Ingres paper comes in a variety of colours in single sheets and pads. Canson M1-teintes paper is also good for writing on and is slightly thicker than the Ingres. You can now also get a range of papers incorporating plants and other fibrous materials. Many of these are excellent for writing on and give an interesting textured background.

If you feel a less solid background would be more

USING COLOURED INKS

Coloured inks have a limited use with pen-written scripts as many of them contain agents that clog the pen, and the colours tend to fade quickly. However, improvements to inks are continually being made and it may be worth trying some.

For work of a more ephemeral nature, dramatic effects can be achieved with inks used in conjunction with automatic pens. These are ideal for poster work, as they come in larger widths than pen nibs that are fitted on to a pen holder.

You should fill the pen from the side and keep the serrated edge of the nib uppermost when you are writing. It will help the flow of the ink if you alter the angle of the writing board so it is less steep. Gouache and watercolour can also be used with automatic pens.

Coloured inks also have a use when writing with masking fluid, which acts as a 'resist'. Use masking fluid to write out your words and then leave until dry. Brush over the writing with coloured inks, leave to dry and then rub off the masking fluid (you can rub it off with your finger). When the masking fluid is removed the letters will show up white, or whatever colour background you wrote on. Remember to wash pens and brushes in soapy water.

Coloured inks over masking fluid

suitable for your text, you can paint a flat watercolour wash over white paper with a large, soft paintbrush. Or you can achieve a mottled effect by dabbing on colour while the paper is damp. Watercolour paper is available in sheets or blocks. Blocks glued on all edges eliminate the need for stretching the paper. You will need to stretch single sheets of paper by dampening them and sticking them to a board with tape. Wait until the paper is completely dry again before applying your colour wash.

Once the paper is ready to write on, dust the surface with ground gum sandarac (see Making a gum sandarac pad, overleaf). Brush off any excess. Alternatively, spray the surface of the paper with fixative.

Gouache on Canson MI-teintes paper

Watercolour on a watercolour-washed background

BASIC PRINCIPLES

1 Another idea for a background is to add a crayoned effect after the writing has been done.

2 In this example the lettering is done in gouache on a pastel background. Other backgrounds can be achieved by rubbing pastels over the surface and merging in with cotton wool. Spray with fixative before writing on it.

CHANGING COLOUR IN THE WRITING

how does your garden grow ?

Colour can be changed randomly throughout the text. We have used this technique in the project on the following pages.

SPRING SUMMER AUTUMN WINTER

You can make the colours merge while writing the text by using an automatic pen and feeding a different colour into each side.

Colour can change at the beginning of each new line. Remember to wash and clean the nib before each colour.

SPRING SUMMER AUTUMN WINTER

Write the text with a pale watercolour or watery gouache and add touches of stronger colour to the letter while the paint is still wet. Use a small, pointed brush of good quality, such as sable.

MAKING A GUM SANDARAC PAD

A gum sandarac pad is used to rub over the surface of painted paper to prepare it for lettering.

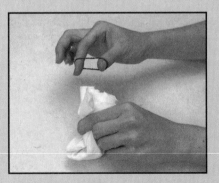

Grind about 2 tablespoonsful of gum sandarac to a very fine powder with a mortar and pestle.

Pour the powdered sandarac on to the centre of a small piece of white cotton. Draw up the ends of the cloth and fasten them with a rubber band.

P R O J E C T

NURSERY RHYME

1 Write out the words in the italic hand on layout paper with black ink using different sizes of nib at different x-heights. Do not worry about positioning the text in any particular way at this stage. A number 3 nib at an x-height of 5 nib-widths and a number 2½ nib at 4 nib-widths have been used here, and the latter chosen to complete the project as it gives a slightly heavier weight letter.

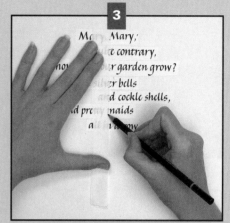

4 Rule up on layout paper and write out the text in black ink according to your layout. This will act as a guide when you write on the coloured background.

5 The background in this project is watercolour, using a mixture of watercolour washes on watercolour paper and wet-in-wet technique with drops of colour splattered on from the brush. Remember, this will act as a background to the writing and should not be dominant.

THE WORDS

Mary, Mary, quite contrary, how does your garden grow? With silver bells and cockle shells and pretty maids all in a row.

2 After you have written out the text, it is a good idea to photocopy it or, if this is not convenient, write it out again. Then, when you are moving the words around to find a pleasing layout, you can stick down the one you think most suitable and then carry on trying different arrangements with the other copy.

3 When you have finalised your layout, measure the inter-line spaces (see step 7 page 17) — they may not all be equal, as you have positioned them by eye. Choose one of the measurements and use this as your inter-line spacing throughout.

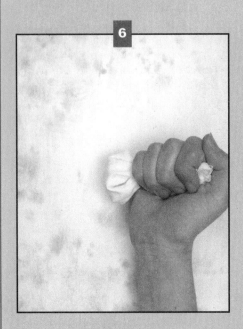

6 Once you have prepared your background, rule up. Keep the pencil lines as faint as you can, as it will not be easy to erase them without taking off some of the background colour. If you do have to rub out, rub gently in a circular motion. Dust the surface with sandarac as described on page 699.

7 Mix the colours for the text, keeping the colours fairly close together in tone and making the changes subtle. Too drastic a contrast would not be appropriate in this case as it would make the text too harsh. We have used mixtures of gouache in

ultramarine, cerulean blue, alizarin crimson, cadmium yellow and white.

8 Write out the text in gouache with the number 2½ nib, using your black and white layout as a guide.

9 Once your text is dry, or before if you are very careful, add dashes of brighter colour to the background with a pointed brush or with the nib used for the text. Choose a larger sized nib to give marks of various thicknesses.

There are, of course, endless possibilities for using colour with calligraphy. You probably have your own favourite poem or quotation that you would like to transcribe — and it will almost certainly suggest its own colours to you!

CALLIGRAPHY

DECORATED LETTERS

MATERIALS

To make the illuminated keepsake shown *below left* you will need:

Above, layout paper; 300gsm HP watercolour paper, 38 x 29cm; scissors; 2 pen holders; Rexel/Mitchell nibs no 2½ and 4; 2 reservoirs; pointed drawing nib; pencil; ruler; eraser; pritt stick; black waterproof ink.

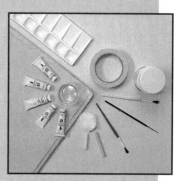

Above, drawing board; masking tape; palette; gouache paints, alizarin crimson, cadmium red, ultramarine, cadmium yellow, white; fixative; soft pastels, green and yellow; jam jar; 2 inexpensive paint brushes; sable paint brush, size 00; piece of cotton wool.

Following on from our earlier lessons on versals and colour and calligraphy, we now show you how you can produce an attractive illuminated keepsake in the style of a medieval manuscript to commemorate a birth.

Decorating capital letters can bring added liveliness to your work, as well as creating a focal point for a block of text or a heading. Decoration need not always involve a complicated approach — sometimes the addition of simple flourishes or washes of watercolour is sufficient.

In this lesson we look at treatments of capitals suitable for use with the different scripts you have been learning. Some are best kept simple. For example, the uncial hand has a roundness and solidity which would would be lost with over-elaboration.

Versal letters lend themselves to the use of a variety of decoration. For our project we use an elaborate approach to illuminating a versal letter using the types of motifs and borders found in medieval manuscripts as a basis for the design.

You can see old manuscripts with their brilliantly gilded and coloured initials in museums and larger libraries. Postcards and books will provide reference for further study at home. A common abbreviation of the word 'manuscript' you may come across during your research is MS.

Some experience and knowledge of working with colour in calligraphy is necessary for this project, so it is advisable that you at least read the lesson on colour and calligraphy (see page 31) before undertaking our project.

DECORATIVE TREATMENTS

The examples on this page illustrate how decorated letters can be used with various scripts. In each case a different treatment has been used for the same name.

1 A simple method of adding decorative colour to letters is by colouring the spaces around the letters. The foundational hand has large counter spaces and lends itself to this type of decorative treatment. After writing the letters, apply watercolour washes with a fine brush in a range of pastel hues in the spaces between the letters and in the counter spaces.

2 Italic capitals can be flourished to add a decorative element. The flourishes should extend naturally from the letters.

3 Gothic capitals are more effective when used as single initials, rather than for a whole word where legibility may be lost through their complexity. Additional dots and fine lines of a contrasting colour can be added.

1

2

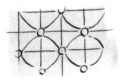
3

VERSALS

These examples illustrate some of the ways that versals can be decorated. These decorated letters are very effective when used for words or blocks of text, and they can be used as an initial letter with most other hands.

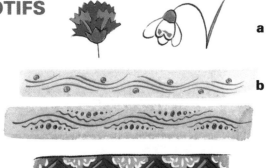

Open versals can be written with strokes of two different colours, using two pens.

These open versals were written in one colour, and when dry, a different colour was used to fill the spaces with decorative dots and zig-zags.

Filled-in versals are written here in one colour, and when dry a larger pen is used to draw a diamond shape in a contrasting colour (or you could use gold gouache). You may need to touch up the colour with a small brush.

These versals were drawn very lightly with a crayon, and then the background was coloured by hatching with crayons of two contrasting colours.

DECORATIVE MOTIFS

The designs we have used for the project (an illuminated keepsake) are derived from, or based on, examples of decoration that may be found in old manuscripts. We have used stylised drawings of flowers that are related to the birthday month: carnations and snowdrops, **a**. A simple linear border crosses the top and bottom, **b**. A more elaborate border has been adapted for use in the body of the letter, **c**. The background pattern is a geometric design, which can be drawn with a drawing pen nib or a fine brush, **d**.

Colours in medieval manuscripts were brilliant and strong, but for the subject of our project a softer approach is better and so the colours are more muted.

The choice of a predominantly pink colour scheme was suggested by the birthstone, which is garnet, and the green was introduced for contrast.

a

b

c

d

INSPIRATION FROM MANUSCRIPTS

By studying medieval manuscripts you will see that various types of decoration were used at different periods. A beautiful manuscript in the British

Museum is the Lindisfarne Gospel, written circa AD 698. It includes some elaborate knotwork designs and some letters that are simply surrounded by small dots, as in this example of the letter A. This approach would also be suitable for the uncial hand (*above*).

PROJECT

ILLUMINATED KEEPSAKE

THE TEMPLATE

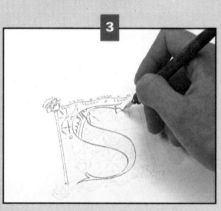

1 Photocopy the template at 119% and trace it in pencil on layout paper (or draw your own letter).

2 Decide on your lettering. Here we have used the italic hand; the name is written with a no 2½ nib, and the text is written with a no 4 nib. Set about writing the text in the usual way — writing it in black ink on layout paper and cutting it up to position it correctly (see page 22, steps 1 and 2). When you are satisfied, stick it down in the appropriate position around your pencilled design. Jot down the measurements of the x-height and the interline spacing.

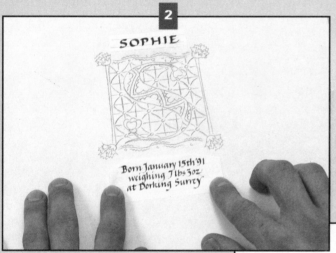

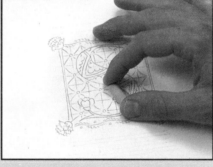

3 Choose a piece of paper for your finished piece. We used a good quality HP watercolour paper, about 300gsm weight, which does not require stretching. Transfer the design on to the paper by rubbing a pencil over the back of the design and then tracing the outline. Go over the outline of the drawing with a pointed nib and watered-down black ink. This heavier line will make the pattern easier to follow when painting. When dry, rub out the pencil line.

4 Using the measurements from your paste-up design, lightly rule up the writing lines on the paper. Rub yellow pastel over the background of the letter and then smudge the colour with a piece of cotton wool. Repeat with the green pastel, then spray with fixative.

5 Mix three tones (light, mid and dark) of pink and green paint to the consistency of thin cream. To do this, mix up plenty of mid-tone pink from white, a small amount of cadmium red and a touch of alizarin crimson. Divide the paint into three parts. Make a light tone by gradually adding a little white gouache and make a dark tone by adding a little more alizarin crimson. Mix green tones in the same way, using white and a touch of ultramarine and cadmium yellow for the mid tone. Add white for the light tone, and more blue and yellow for the dark tone.

6 Write out the text at this stage. In this way, you avoid the risk of making a mistake with the lettering after the elaborate initial is done, and can start again if necessary. We used the mid-tone pink for the writing.

7 Apply a thin wash of watered-down mid-tone pink with the sable brush to areas of the letter and the flowers (not the background pattern). Paint in the green areas in the same way. This stage will clarify the colour plan. Leave to dry.

8 Now apply first the green and then the pink mid-tones with the sable brush, working fairly quickly; if you allow the paint to dry out as you work on large areas, a mark or ridge will appear. If you are righthanded, work from the top lefthand corner to the bottom right, and vice versa if you are lefthanded. Stir the paint with the brush in the palette from time to time, to prevent the colour from separating. When dry, paint in the geometric design.

9 Apply the green and pink light tones and leave to dry.

10 Use white gouache to paint the snowdrops and the dots on the background. Then apply the pink and green dark tones to the design. Leave to dry.

11 When all the paint is thoroughly dry, outline the snowdrop with the mid-tone green. Mix some white gouache to a thicker consistency, and add the fine lines and dots which give detail to the design and create highlights. Finally, mix some dark tone green paint fairly thickly and add the fine dark outlines.

Decide on the margin of white space that you want around your birthday keepsake and choose a mount of a toning colour. You could buy a ready-made frame, or have one specially made.

CALLIGRAPHY

COPPERPLATE

In this lesson we introduce you to Copperplate, an elegant script developed in the 17th century, and show you how to use it to letter a special recipe and an attractive label for a gift pack of a homemade preserve.

In Copperplate we have a very different hand from those so far studied. The thick and thin strokes are not made by a square edged pen, but by pressure and the release of pressure on a pointed flexible nib.

This style of writing, which has its roots in the italic hands of the 15th and 16th centuries, developed in England in the 17th century. It takes its name from a form of printing. Fine lines were engraved into a thin copper plate with a pointed steel burin. The plate was then inked, wiped clean and pressed on to paper. Mistakes on the plate could be burnished away and corrections made. This meant the page when printed could be far more precise and regular than the original writing on which it was based, and extremely elaborate curves and flourishes could be added.

Gradually pen-made letters began to imitate the engraved ones and the script came to be called Copperplate writing.

English Round Hand

Copperplate is also known as English Round Hand. Being fairly quick to write and very legible, it became the normal hand for business and record keeping. It survived in this capacity all through the 19th century and was still being taught in some schools well into the 20th century.

The main characteristics of Copperplate are the invariably thick downward strokes, very thin up strokes and a marked forward slope of approximately 55°. Each letter appears to lead effortlessly into the next, though in practice they are made up of separate strokes.

GUIDE SHEET

To make your own guide sheet use A3 paper. Rule the top line, then mark 6mm down for the ascender height, 4mm for the x-height and 6mm for the descender. Set the dividers 16mm apart (the distance between one ascender line and the next) and use them to rule up (see page 298 'Ruling up with dividers', second paragraph).

To add the 55° diagonal lines place the protractor on the bottom left corner of the sheet with the 0° line along the bottom and the 90° line up the side. Mark 55° and rule it in.

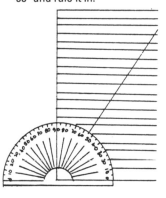

Place your ruler along the diagonal line and draw in parallel lines. If the ruler is wide you may wish to add extra lines in between. Be very accurate when you are doing this.

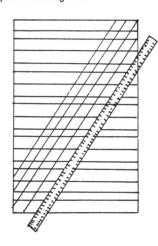

This example of Copperplate *right* comes from *The Universal Penman*, a collection of examples of writing by leading penmen of the mid-18th century put together by George Bickham. A paperback facsimile of this book is published by Dover Books.

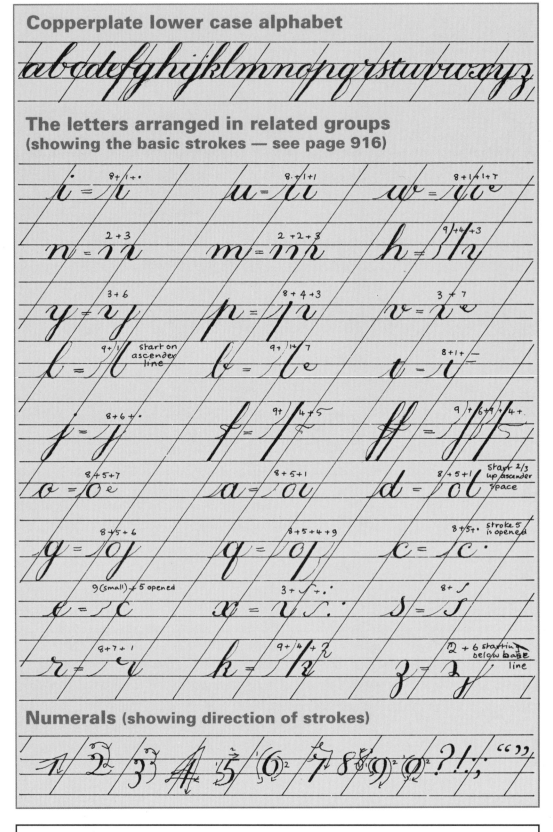

Copperplate lower case alphabet

The letters arranged in related groups
(showing the basic strokes — see page 916)

Numerals (showing direction of strokes)

Copperplate capitals

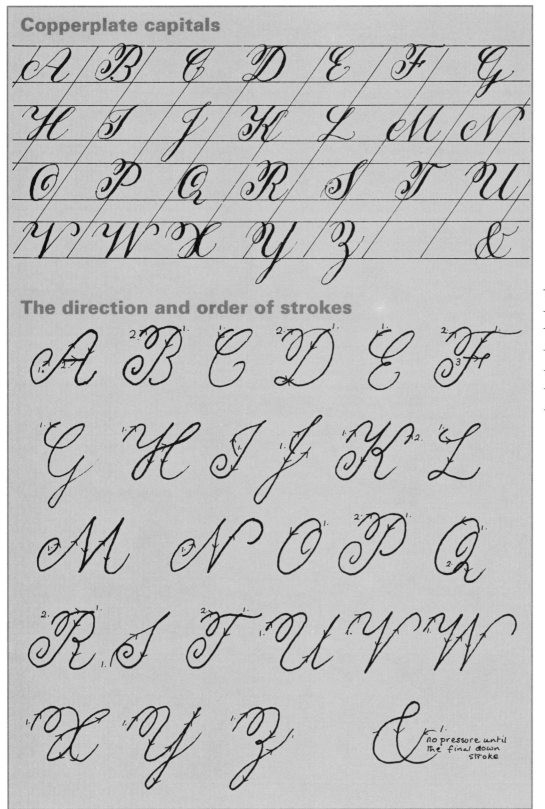

The direction and order of strokes

no pressure until the final down stroke

LINE SPACING

In Copperplate there is no nib width measurement, because the nib is pointed. The x-height is calculated in relation to the ascender and descender height in the following ratio: ascender 3: x-height 2: descender 3. In this project the x-height is 4mm and ascenders and descenders are 6mm. Do not attempt to write smaller than this until you are more experienced. There is usually no extra space between the ascenders of one line and descenders of the next.

RULES

1 The nib must always point along the 55° slope line.
2 Downward strokes are always thick.
3 Upward strokes are always thin.
4 There is a constant slope to the writing of 55° so all straight lines should look parallel.
5 All ovals, spirals and loops have their axis along the 55° slope line.
6 Always use smooth paper so that the nib does not catch the paper.

Below: How capital letters and lower case letters fit together on the guide sheet.

HOW TO MAKE THE STROKES

To make thick strokes apply pressure to open the point of the pen, then pull down (see **A** below).

Upward strokes are made with the minimum amount of pressure (see **B** below). At first you may find the nib catches in the paper, but with practice you will find you can avoid this.

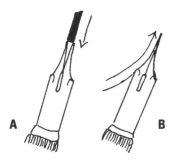

Larger writing requires more pressure to make a wider stroke, but the same nib can be used for any size of writing.

WRITING TOOLS

The acute slope of the lettering and the need to keep the nib pointing along that slope means that most people find an elbowed nib, or a straight nib in an elbowed holder, the best tool to use (see *below*). No reservoir is needed.

The Gillott 303 and 404 are good straight nibs. There are many other straight pointed nibs available, but make sure that the nib is flexible and not rigid before you buy one. It helps to keep the pen at the right 55° angle if you slope the paper even when using an angled pen or nib (*bottom*).

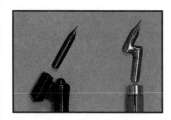

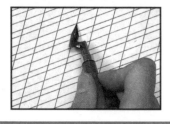

BASIC STROKES for the lower case alphabet

Lower case letters are made up from nine basic strokes plus one or two minor additions. Practise these strokes until you can do them easily and correctly before you make a start on the letters.

1 Place nib on waist line; press, then hold for a moment before pulling downwards. Gradually release pressure as nib curves to the right. Continue upwards parallel to down stroke.

2 Begin with no pressure. Gradually increase it after curving to the right. Maintain pressure to end of stroke to ensure a square and not a pointed end.

3 This stroke begins as stroke 2 and ends as stroke 1.

4 Apply pressure at top of stroke, hold for a moment to make a square top. Maintain pressure finishing as in stroke 2.

5 This stroke is an oval with its axis on the 55° slope of the writing. Begin with nib at 2 o'clock and move round anti-clockwise, increasing pressure as you go down the left side and releasing it as you begin to curve round the bottom. This curve and the top curve should be the same as those in 1, 2 and 3.

6 Begin as in stroke 4 but start at waist line. Just before reaching descender line release pressure and curve to left. Continue upwards crossing the downstroke just below the base line. Finish with a very slight reverse curve.

7 Begin with a tiny anti-clockwise circle. Release pressure as you curve round to the right.

8 A gently curving upward hair-line stroke sloping slightly more than the slope of writing.

9 Repeat stroke 8 and add a second curve in the same direction up to the ascender line. Use minimal pressure for strokes 8 and 9.

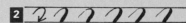

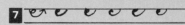

BASIC STROKES for capitals

1 A downward stroke. Begin with little pressure. Gradually increase it and then gradually decrease it curving slightly to the left.

2 Begin as stroke 1 and finish with a spiral to the left. Note that the axis is along the 55° slope.

3 A steeper version of 1. It is used in M, N, W and V.

4 An anti-clockwise spiral which leads into A, M and N.

5 Lead in at the top of B, D, F, P, R, T, X, U and Y.

6 Lead in to C, E, G and L.

7 Similar to basic stroke 3 of lower case alphabet. Lead into H, K, W and V.

P R O J E C T

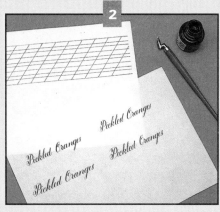

1 Place an A3 guide sheet behind A3 layout paper and fasten them together with masking tape. Write out your chosen recipe, omitting the title. Allow a margin of approximately 5cm, but do not worry too much about the position on the page at this stage.

2 Rule up a wider guide sheet for the heading. The spaces between the lines should measure 9mm: 6mm: 9mm. You will only need to rule a few lines. Now write out the heading several times.

GUIDE SHEET AND TEMPLATE

You can use your own guide sheet or reproduce this one by photocopying it at 200% and then again at 200%. Photocopy the template for the label at 200%.

3 Lightly rule in a vertical central line on another sheet of layout paper. Using scissors cut out the recipe heading, ingredients and method and position on the layout paper, making sure the heading and ingredients are centred (see page 17) and that the margin is the same width on either side. Leave a space equivalent to one writing line between heading and ingredients, and ingredients and method. Dab the back of your recipe pieces with cow gum and stick in place.

4 Using the pasted-up version as a guide, stick the wider guide sheet for the heading on to the main guide sheet with cow gum. Then attach another sheet of layout paper to your guide sheet and secure with masking tape.

HELPFUL HINT

If you are using an elbowed pen-holder transfer ink to a small jar with a wide neck. You cannot dip the pen into a normal ink bottle.

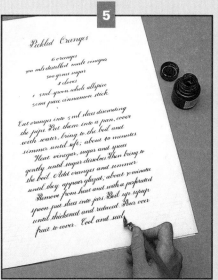

5 Check that you have enough lines on the guide sheet for the whole of your recipe before beginning to write it out.

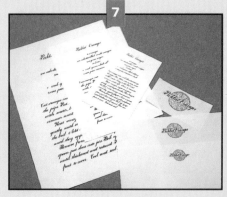

7 Reduce the recipe on a photocopier to A5. Reduce the label to a size to fit your jar.

6 To make the label either photocopy the template or design your own using the title of your recipe. Use the compass and pencil to draw the shape of the orange slice and the fine black fibre-tip pen to draw over your pencil outlines.

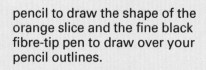

8 Colour the orange slice on the label using the watercolour pencil. Gently go over your orange pencil marks with a fine watercolour brush.

9 On the wrong side of the cotton fabric use a compass and pencil to draw a circle measuring twice the diameter of the lid of the jar of pickled oranges. Cut out the circle with pinking shears. Fold the recipe, place it on the lid and cover with the cotton circle. Secure with a rubber band and then tie with ribbon.

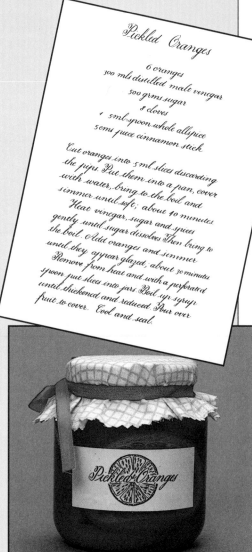

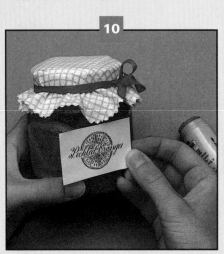

10 Stick your label on the jar of pickled oranges with UHU or a similar adhesive and you will have a most attractive gift.

Copperplate is an extremely fluid and elegant script which relies on a light touch. If your pen catches in the paper and won't move easily, check that you are not gripping it too tightly.

MONOGRAM STAMP

Drawing on the calligraphy skills you have already learned, we show you in this project how to go about designing your own monogram. It is then a simple matter to transform this into a personal rubber stamp that you can print on your writing paper, envelopes and other stationery.

MATERIALS

To make the rubber stamp show *below left* you will need:

Above, HB pencil; A4 paper; tracing paper; fine black waterproof felt-tip pen; hard rubber eraser, 4.5 x 3.5cm.

Above, needle; pin vice; small craft knife or scalpel; lino-cutting holder and V-shaped tool size 1; inked stamp pad; piece of wood, 4 x 3 x 2cm; impact adhesive.

A monogram is a sign composed of letterforms that are usually all the letters of a name, or the initial letters of someone's name.

The Greeks were the original inventors of the monogram, and many of the early Greek and Roman coins show the monograms of rulers and towns. By the Middle Ages monograms were being designed for ecclesiastical, artistic and commercial use. They were often used by the early printers, and are important in establishing the origin of early printed books. They were also used by painters, engravers and ceramicists. Medieval merchants used monograms — composed of their initials and a special device — to mark their goods.

Making your mark

A monogram device was part of the royal seal used in the Middle Ages by the monarch to authenticate documents. Seals were also used by lesser people such as merchants and clerics to mark documents and goods. In later times people sealed their documents with sealing wax, and stamped the seal while still warm with a signet ring.

More recently, rubber stamps have become popular. Most offices have some kind of a rubber stamp, probably a date stamp, which is used with an inked stamp pad. Specially made rubber stamps can incorporate the company logo, which may consist of a special identifying device based on the company's initials. When designing a monogram the constituent letters may be reversed, or arranged in such a complicated way that it may be difficult to identify them (see **a**, *below right*).

Personal monogram stamp

It's an exciting exercise to design your own personal monogram. The letterforms can be modified to make them fit together into a satisfying shape. This need not be a rectangle — you could make it square or circular, as long as it fits on your chosen rubber eraser. When you have made your stamp, you can use it on your letterhead, cards, tags, and even wrapping paper.

MONOGRAM IDEAS

You can look for books on monograms in your local library to give you ideas. The monogram, **a**, for the name Nikolaus is based on an early Christian design and was re-drawn by Rudolf Koch (a 20th-century German calligrapher and type designer) for his *Book of Signs* (Dover Publications). The intertwined M and U, **b**, is an example of an elaborate Victorian design, with fanciful serifs and a three-dimensional effect (from *Monograms and Alphabetic Devices* by Hayward and Blanche Cirker, Dover Publications).

DESIGNING A MONOGRAM

Here we show you some of the many approaches you can take to designing a monogram from two letters. The size and shape of your rubber stamp will determine the proportions and scale of your design. We have used the letters V and M and our eraser measures 4.5 x 3.5cm.

1 A useful starting point for designing a monogram is to consider the essential form of the letters. In their skeleton Roman capital form (see page 28), drawn here with a fine felt-tip pen, we identify the strong diagonal elements of the letters and the fact that the shape of the V is the central structure of the M.

2 Consider the scripts already learned. These four examples show the use of italic (see page 14): **a** and **b**, two variations of flourished capitals (see page 38) using an edged pen; **c**, a version drawn with coloured double pencils (see page 25) linking the letters, using the V at a smaller size; **d**, lower case letters.

3 With uncial letters (see page 24) there is a strong contrast between the diagonal form of the V and the rounded M.

4 In these versal letters (see page 29) the V has been made to fit into the corresponding shape of the M, forming a harmonious unit.

INVENTING FORMS

You might like to consider more fanciful or abstract letter forms.
a These letters are drawn and then painted. The wavy forms give fluidity to the movement of the diagonals.
b A drawn design which uses the triangle within the V and repeats this to suggest a variation of the M.
c Skeleton forms, with a high centre to the M, are given an amusing graphic quality with large dots at the joins and ends of the stems.

BORDERS

A border design may enhance a monogram design. If the design is for a square or rectangular shape, pay special attention to the corners and make sure that your design is balanced.

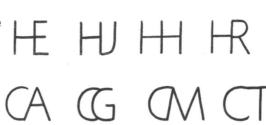

TYPEFACES

Typefaces can provide a good source of inspiration for a design. These letterforms were traced from a bold version of Gill Sans, a typeface designed by Eric Gill, who was also a lettercutter and stone sculptor.

OTHER LETTER COMBINATIONS

These examples of other letter combinations illustrate a variety of solutions to combining skeleton letters of different basic shapes. You will see that in their skeleton form, letterforms are essentially triangular, round or rectangular, with

lines that are diagonal, horizontal, vertical or curved. Letterforms can be combined to share stems (as in HE), and forms can be used in their mirror image (as in AA). Different scripts will, of course, create different shapes and lines, as you have already seen.

P R O J E C T

THE TEMPLATE

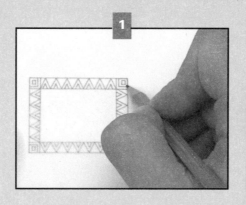

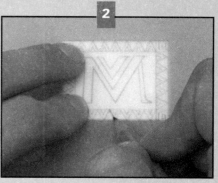

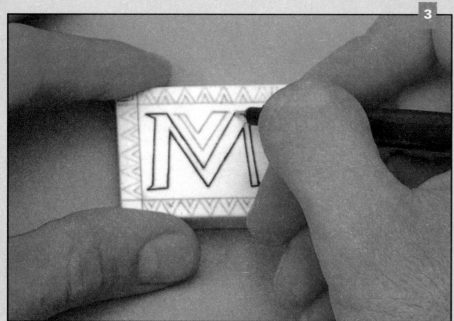

1 Make a careful finished drawing of your monogram design, remembering that it must fit the size of the eraser. Trace the border design from the template using an HB pencil and a piece of tracing paper. Position your monogram design centrally within the border design and trace it.

2 Turn the tracing paper over and position it accurately on the eraser. Holding it firmly to prevent it from slipping, carefully draw over the lines of the design with the pencil to transfer the drawing in reverse on to the eraser.

3 Remove the tracing paper and carefully draw over the lines with a fine felt-tip pen, in order to give crisp cutting guidelines.

HELPFUL HINTS

Remember that the drawing must be made in reverse on the eraser, so that the printing will give the correct image.

If you cannot obtain a pin vice, you can improvise by inserting the head of the needle in a cork. You do need some kind of holder for the needle to make it easier to handle.

4 Secure the needle in the pin vice. Gradually working towards yourself, use the needle to score the outline lightly, making sure you angle the point of the needle away from the edge of your design to prevent undercutting it. Remember that you can trim away any surplus rubber later, but there is no way to replace a piece that you have cut away by accident.

5 Holding the V-shaped tool at a shallow angle to the eraser, carefully cut around the outline again, making sure that you don't undercut the design itself.

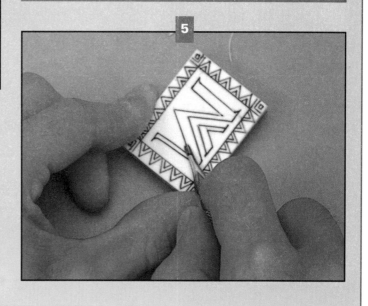

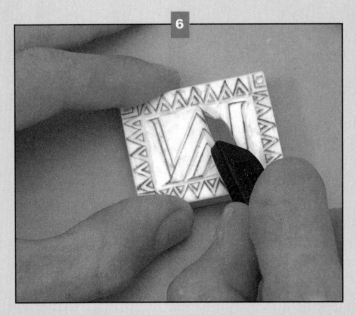

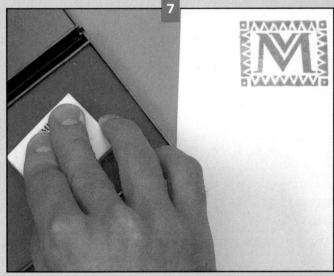

6 Cut away the background to your design with a scalpel. If you need to make tiny additional cuts around your design you may find it easier to use the V-shaped tool.

7 Press the eraser on to the inked stamp pad, place a sheet of paper on a flat surface and make a trial print of the design. Check the accuracy of the design, and make sure that the background is clean. Make any final cutting adjustments if necessary.

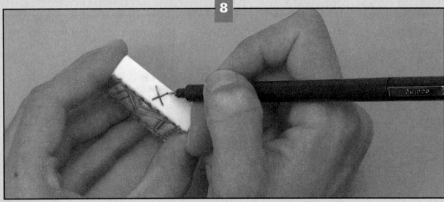

HELPFUL HINT

When printing with an ink pad, press the stamp firmly on to the paper, without wobbling the stamp from side to side. Re-ink between stampings or the tone of print will fade. If you don't have an ink pad you can use a felt-tip pen to go over your design before you print.

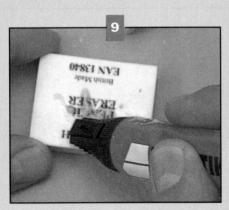

8 Mark the top edge of your eraser with a felt-tip pen to show which way up you should print the design.

9 Apply the glue following the manufacturer's instructions to the back of the eraser and stick to the block of wood (which should be a little smaller than the eraser so that you can easily see the mark you have drawn). This will form a handle for your stamp.

HELPFUL HINT

If you can't find a piece of wood already cut to size for the handle, buy a small piece of balsa wood as this is softer and easier to cut with a small saw. Balsa wood can be bought from most hardware or art-supply shops.

Stamp pads are available in a variety of colours. Once you have finished using the stamp, clean it with a damp sponge and dry it with a soft cloth. Don't be tempted to scrub it with a brush as this could wear away your stamp.

CALLIGRAPHY

HANDMADE PENS

The type of pen you use for calligraphy has a profound effect on the marks that you produce. In this project we show you how to make three different pens from everyday household materials — garden cane, card with cloth, and veneer — and demonstrate how they can be used to produce three highly decorative alphabet designs.

Ancient Egyptian scribes cut their pens from reeds, and in the Middle Ages the scribes in the monasteries cut quill pens from the flight feathers of geese and other large birds to produce their elaborate illuminated manuscripts. It is only since the 18th century that pens manufactured from steel have provided calligraphers with ready-made writing tools.

Our cane pen is based on the ancient method of cutting a reed pen, with the modification of a metal reservoir to hold more ink. Garden cane makes a suitable material, but if you have bamboo growing in your garden, or live near an area where reeds or rushes grow, you could try these. Freshly cut materials are easier to cut than garden cane and will have more flexibility.

A pen made from card and an all-purpose cloth may not look beautiful or traditional, but it can be made to any size and will encourage you to use a loose, free action when making marks on paper. The cloth holds a lot of ink and is therefore suitable for writing very large letters.

A piece of veneer slotted into the end of a piece of cane makes a very sensitive flexible pen. Odd scraps of veneer can usually be obtained from furniture restorers or makers, or from craft shops. You could use balsa wood in place of veneer, and this, being less flexible, will produce different marks; as it is also a softer wood, it will not last as long. This type of pen can be made very wide.

Try out the pens on papers with different textures. You will notice that each pen has its own individual 'touch'. We have used the pens to design some attractive alphabet panels. As your involvement with calligraphy grows, you will probably feel increasingly intrigued by the design and arrangement of letters and will want to create your own alphabet panel.

MATERIALS

To make the pens shown *below left* you will need:

Above, general equipment: craft knife; scissors; cutting mat; masking tape. *For the cane pen:* 15cm garden cane, 1cm diameter; small craft knife; bradawl; aluminium can. *For cloth and card pen:* piece of strong card, 3 x 10cm, 1mm thick; all-purpose cloth; pencil. *For the veneer pen:* small piece of veneer; 15cm garden cane; fine sandpaper.

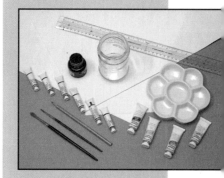

Above, for alphabet design page 53: sheet of NOT watercolour paper; black ink; watercolour brushes, sizes 6 and 2; watercolour paints, red, blue, yellow, orange, green and purple. *For alphabet design page 54, top:* sheet of HP watercolour paper; gouache paints, burnt sienna and orange. *For alphabet design page 54, bottom right:* sheet of NOT watercolour paper; gouache paints, grey and red. *General equipment:* pencil; ruler; water jar; brush; palette.

P R O J E C T

CANE PEN

You will need: cutting mat; small and large craft knife; scissors; 15cm garden cane; bradawl; aluminium can.

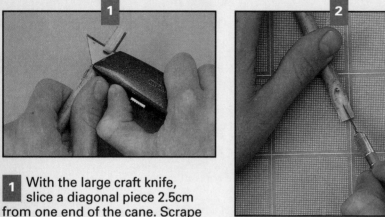

1 With the large craft knife, slice a diagonal piece 2.5cm from one end of the cane. Scrape the pith from the inside of the cane with the small knife and the bradawl.

2 Lay the cane on a cutting mat as shown, and with the small craft knife make a slit about 1cm long along the centre of the projecting piece.

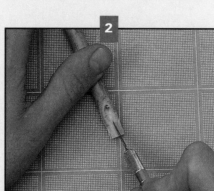

3 Cut a small piece from both sides of the diagonal cut until you achieve the width you want for your nib (take care that the knife doesn't slip and cut your hand).

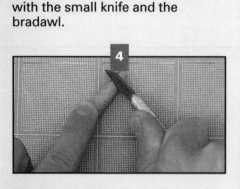

4 Place the nib on the cutting mat and make small diagonal cuts to pare down the rounded top of the cane to a thin edge. Do not take off too much or the nib will begin to disintegrate.

HELPFUL HINT

If anything goes wrong when you are cutting the pen, simply re-cut it, starting further up the cane, or cut the other end.

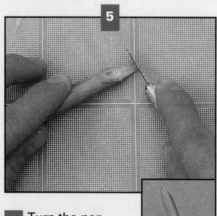

5 Turn the pen over and cut the tip off the end with a vertical cut. To make a left-handed pen, cut it at the angle shown (inset).

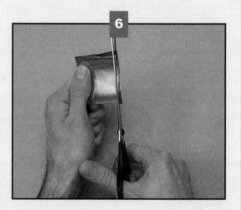

6 Make a starter hole with the bradawl in an aluminium can and with scissors cut a rectangle of metal. Then cut a strip about 3cm long, and slightly narrower than the width of the nib.

7 To make a reservoir, bend one end of the strip into a U-shape as shown, and curve the other end slightly. Push the U-shaped end into the pen. The other end should touch the nib about 3mm from the tip. If it does not fit, trim back the metal strip, or dig out more pith.

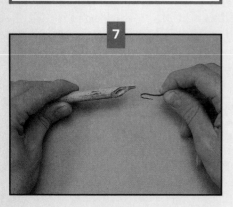

8 Dip the pen into ink and test it on a piece of paper. The ink tends to run dry very quickly and gives a tonal effect, and this is part of the charm of these pens.

CANE PEN ALPHABET PANEL

In this panel we have contrasted strong dark Gothic letters with colourful watercolour washes. First, smooth a piece of damp NOT watercolour paper on to a board and secure with tape. When dry, draw a series of rectangles lightly in pencil and flood the shapes that do not touch with clean water using a size 6 brush. While still wet, use a smaller brush to apply a thin line of thickly loaded watercolour just inside the edge, using a different colour for each rectangle. The colour will spread inwards leaving a sharp outline. Leave to dry, then treat any overlapping shapes in the same way. When dry, take the paper off the board. Using black ink and the cane pen, freely write the letters of the Gothic alphabet (see page 20) in the shapes to create a balanced design.

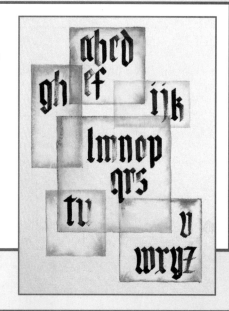

CLOTH AND CARD PEN

You will need: cutting mat; card, 3 x 10cm; all-purpose cloth; masking tape; scissors; craft knife; pencil.

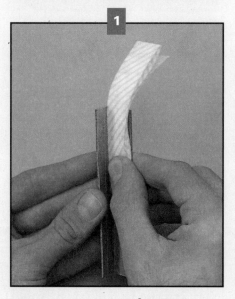

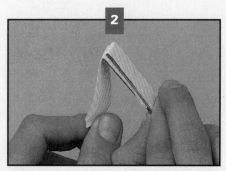

2 Fold the ends of the cloth back over the card each side, making sure the pieces of card are level.

1 With a craft knife, cut the card into two pieces, each 1.5 x 10cm. With scissors, cut a strip of all-purpose cloth 1.5 x 35cm. Fold the cloth strip in half twice and sandwich 4cm of the folded end between the two pieces of card.

3 Wrap a strip of masking tape around the card and cloth as tightly as possible, about 1.5cm from the end. Add another strip to secure the cloth to the card.

4 To produce a 3-stroke nib, place the pen on the cutting mat and with a very sharp craft knife cut 2 V-shaped notches, about 3mm wide. To make a 2-stroke nib, cut one V-shaped notch. It is important to make a straight cut through all the layers.

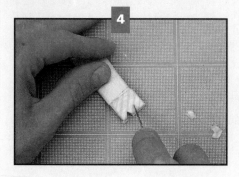

5 The pen is easier to hold if you attach a handle. This can be made by securing a pencil to it with masking tape. Dip the pen into gouache paint and make some marks. With use, these pens tend to lose their sharpness, but they can be dried and used again. The two sides of this 2-stroke nib have been dipped in gouache paints of different colours to give the effect of a shadowed line.

ALPHABET WITH CLOTH AND CARD PEN AND CANE PEN

In this alphabet panel we have superimposed two different letterforms using two pens. Using HP watercolour paper, first write out the alphabet in lower case italic letters (see page 14) with a cane pen and burnt sienna gouache. (The pigment gives an uneven cover which can be used

to advantage.) When dry, write the word ALPHABET over the alphabet in large italic capitals using a 3-stroke cloth and card pen and orange gouache.

VENEER PEN

You will need: cutting mat; masking tape; 15cm garden cane; craft knife; small piece of veneer; fine sandpaper.

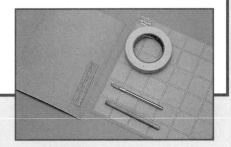

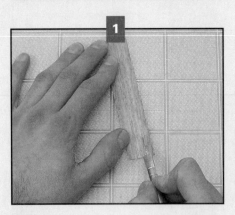

1 With a craft knife cut a piece of veneer 5mm x 3cm with the wood grain running along the length of the piece. Sharpen one end as finely as possible with sandpaper.

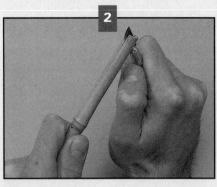

2 Cut a slit across one end of the cane to a depth of about 4cm, taking care not to split the whole length of the cane.

ALPHABET WITH VENEER PEN

Here we have used rounded uncial forms, arranging the letters to create a harmonious pattern. Try some rough designs with the pen using uncial letters (see page 24). Map out the design in pencil on a piece of watercolour paper. Using grey gouache, write out all the letters except the O, allowing the paint almost to run out before you dip the pen again, thus creating an irregular effect. Wash the pen, then add the O with red gouache.

3 Holding the slit open with the knife, slot in the unsharpened end of the veneer, leaving about 1.5cm projecting at the end. Remove the knife.

4 Bind masking tape as tightly as possible around the cane below the veneer to secure it. This will also prevent the ink from seeping up the cane. Try using the pen with different types of ink, paint and paper. You will find that you have to replenish the pen frequently.

CALLIGRAPHY
BANNER

MATERIALS

To make the banner shown *below left* you will need:

Above, layout pad; palette; 3/8in chisel-edged brush; black ink; gouache paint, various colours; pencil; ruler.

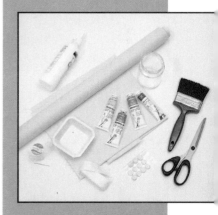

Above, 2.3m unbleached calico; 1m cotton tape; needle and white cotton; roll of decorator's lining paper; PVA medium; 3in decorator's brush; dish or bowl for mixing paint; Blu-Tack; scissors; jam jars; acrylic paints, cadmium red, cobalt blue, ultramarine and cadmium yellow.

In this calligraphy project we show you how to tackle lettering on a large scale to produce a decorative display banner — and introduce you to the technique of writing a bold block capital alphabet with a decorator's paintbrush.

A poster or banner used for advertising or display should be big and bright enough to attract attention, with letterforms that are bold enough to be read easily from a distance.

Chunky capitals
We have lettered our banner for a school summer fair with a 3-inch decorator's brush, which makes a robust writing tool, and have used a block capital alphabet, which has a strong impact.

This alphabet is strongly influenced by the Neuland typeface, designed by the German calligrapher and type designer Rudolf Koch (1874-1934). The underlying form of these letters is simplified to their most basic geometric shapes (see page 28), and the edge of the brush is turned to produce the widest stroke on most parts of the letters. This contradicts the rule that you have already learned for other alphabets, where a generally constant pen angle is maintained.

We show you how to write this alphabet first on a small scale, using a 3/8-inch chisel-edged nylon brush. Unlike the constant line produced by a hard broad-edged nib, the flexible brush responds to pressure and requires some practice and a steady hand in order to achieve even strokes. It does, however, allow you to turn around the curved strokes, which are the trickiest to write. You will probably find it easier to write the letters with the large brush — remember that at a distance a few rough edges will not show.

The design and colour scheme of the banner is worked out first on a small scale, and then written on a large scale on paper to determine the size of the banner. We have used unbleached calico and acrylic paints (which are waterproof) so that the banner can be displayed outdoors. The banner has a spattered background, and we have used two different colours for the strokes of the letters to increase its decorative effect.

GUIDELINES

A Vertical strokes are written with the edge of the brush approximately horizontal to the writing line. Turn the brush to give the widest line on diagonal strokes (except Z).

B For the curved strokes of B, D, P, R and the diagonal stroke of Z, hold the edge of the brush at a constant angle of 10°.

C For the circular letters C, G, O, Q and U, and the curves of E and S, twist the brush to give the fullest width around the curve. The circle of O and Q, and the curve of U, are written in two strokes.

D For the horizontal cross strokes of E, F, and H, hold the edge of the brush at 90° to the writing line.

BLOCK CAPITALS WITH A BRUSH
showing order of strokes

The letters are written at 3 'nib-widths' high using a ³/₈in or 3in brush.

P R O J E C T

1 Work out the layout on a small scale, using the 3/8-inch chisel-edged brush and black ink on layout paper (use an x-height of 3 'nib widths'). Experiment with different colour combinations using gouache.

2 The size of the letters will depend on the distance from which you want the banner to be read. We have used a 3-inch decorator's brush for 9-inch high letters, which makes a banner nearly two and a half metres long. Working on a large table, or on the floor, rule up a sheet of lining paper with minimal space between the lines and write out the words to your chosen layout with the brush and acrylic paint diluted with water (a single colour will suffice at this stage).

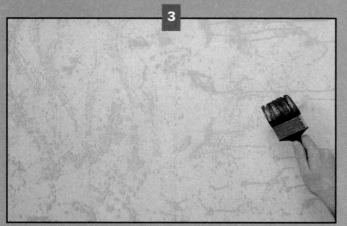

3 Cut the calico to size and sew loops of cotton tape at each corner. Iron out any creases. In a jam jar, mix a 50:50 solution of PVA and water and brush this all over the upper surface of the calico, including the edges (this seals the surface ready for painting and prevents the edges from fraying). Wash the brush. Mix cadmium yellow acrylic paint to a runny consistency and flick this over the fabric with the brush to create a spattered pattern.

4 When the paint has dried, cut out the individual letters from the lining paper and arrange them in position on the calico. To give the message a more lively effect, place the letters so that they are not as rigidly in line as on the original layout.

5 Anchor the letters in place with blobs of Blu-Tack, then lightly draw around the outline of each letter with a soft pencil.

6 In a dish large enough for the 3-inch brush, dilute some cadmium red acrylic paint to the consistency of thin cream. Remove the paper letters and, using the pencil outlines as a guide, paint the red strokes of the letters only. Don't worry about any rough edges — they can be touched up with the smaller brush later if necessary. Leave to dry.

7 Mix cobalt blue acrylic paint as before, adding a small amount of ultramarine blue to make the colour more opaque, and paint the blue strokes of the letters.

8 Add a decorative border along the top and bottom of the banner, as shown.

Thread rope or string through the loops at the corner of the banner and hang it in a prominent place to advertise your summer fair.

CHINESE CALLIGRAPHY

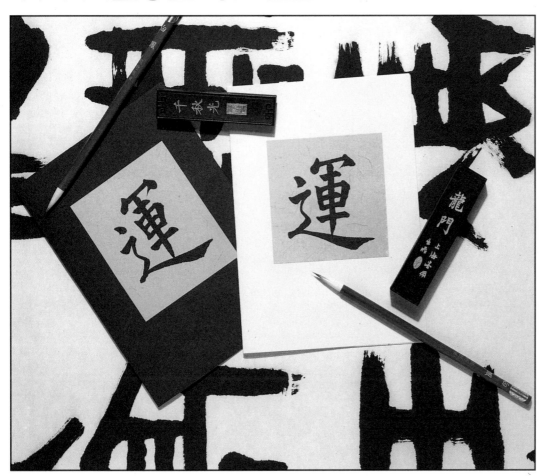

In this lesson Chinese calligrapher Qu Lei Lei introduces you to the ancient art of Chinese calligraphy, which is written with a brush. He shows you basic strokes and techniques, and how to write a 'good luck' greeting.

In China, calligraphy has traditionally been valued as the highest form of visual art. As non-representational art, its impact relies on the dynamic movement of the brush line, which (according to the Chinese) should be infused with *ch'i* — creative or vital energy. The resulting characters are regarded as living entities (see box).

The Chinese do not have an alphabet of 26 letters such as ours, but instead use many thousands of individual characters, each of which represents a word. These have been developed from pictographic characters that had their origins in the second century BC (see page 60).

The characters are written with a pointed, flexible brush, which is always held perpendicular to the paper. The brush is a very subtle and responsive writing tool that enables the calligrapher to imbue his strokes with a sense of direction and movement. There are eight basic brushstrokes used in the Standard form (see page 62). To become proficient with the brush you need plenty of practice.

In this project we show you how to stretch your finished calligraphy so that it is completely smooth. You can obtain the materials needed for Chinese calligraphy by mail order from Guanghwa Co Ltd (tel: 071 831 5888 for further information).

The life within

'Every horizontal line is like a mass of clouds in battle form; every hook like a bent bow of great strength, every dot like a falling rock from a high peak, every turning of the stroke like a brass hook, every drawn-out line like a dry vine of great age and every swift and free stroke like a runner on his start.'

Chinese calligrapher Wang Hsi-chi

MATERIALS

To make the good luck card shown *below left* you will need:

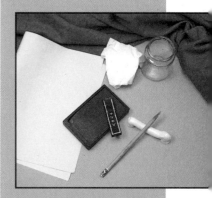

Above, length of felt or old blanket; medium 'white cloud' brush; ink stick; inkstone; brush rest; jam jar; grass paper; tissue.

Above, plywood board; Conté board; flour and water paste (see page 64); large soft hair mounting brush; large bristle mounting brush; palette knife; double-sided adhesive tape; black card 30 x 21cm; jam jar.

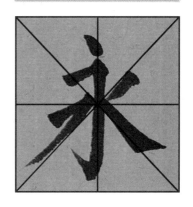

CHARACTER SQUARE

Chinese schoolchildren are taught to write in squares, such as the ones *below*. This helps to centre the character and to achieve good proportions.

Photocopy the square to the size you require for your writing, and place the grid under your writing paper as a guide.

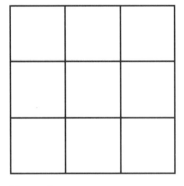

'Mi' (rice) character square

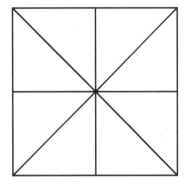

Nine palace square

RHYTHM AND MOVEMENT

In general, characters are built up with strokes that progress from top left to bottom right. The character *below* ('heart') is a good example of how all the parts of a character are related and have a rhythm. In the diagram the black arrows show the brushstrokes (notice how the two dots, top right, 'talk' to each other). The red line indicates the general movement within the character.

DEVELOPMENT OF CHINESE CHARACTERS

The top line *above* shows the pictographic characters for, *from left to right*, wish, fish, bird, woman, horse, water and rain. Dating from 1000-2000 BC, these are the earliest forms — simplified drawings which represent the image of the word.

In the second line are Xiao Zhuan characters, from the Qin Dynasty (221-207BC). There are still strong pictographic characteristics, but the strokes are more stylised.

In the third line are Standard characters, which were developed in the Tang dynasty (618-906 AD) and are still in use today. Although their origins are still recognisable, the forms have become abstracted, and they have become graphic symbols composed of a limited number of basic strokes.

THE TEXT PAGE

Chinese is written in columns, from the top to the bottom of the page, starting at the righthand side of the paper and working to the left.

This text is a well-known poem about the Lu Shau Mountain by Li Bai. The poem starts at top right, and in the left column is the title of the poem and the calligrapher's signature, below which he has stamped his personal seal (or 'chop'). The composition is balanced with a decorative seal, top right.

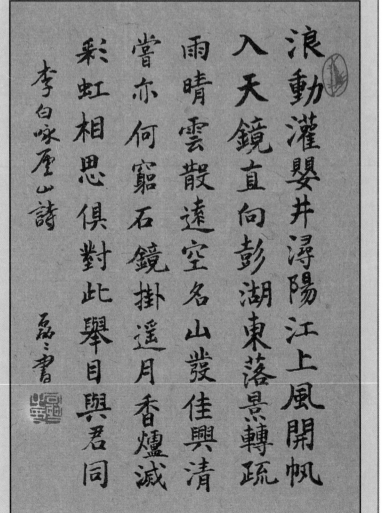

THE FOUR TREASURES

The basic pieces of equipment — the brush, ink stick, paper and inkstone — are known as the four treasures of Chinese calligraphy.

Cover the table with a piece of fabric (such as woollen felt or an old blanket) to provide a good surface to work on (newspaper can be used, but is not as good). If you are righthanded, place the four treasures at the top right of the table.

'Xuan', or rice paper, is suitable for both calligraphy and painting. We have used grass paper (which is straw-coloured) which is much cheaper and good for calligraphy practice.

BRUSH CONTROL

Hold the brush perpendicular to the table. Your thumb and first two fingers should hold the brush, and the fourth and fifth fingers support it. With practice, this allows very sensitive manipulation, which should come from the fingers and the wrist.

The brushstrokes are very subtle, and what appears to be a straight line has some complex movements. There is nearly always a contrary movement at the start and finish of the stroke — all strokes return to the centre. To start with, practise drawing a horizontal line (see diagram for figure 3, page 62).

1 Press the tip of the brush gently on the paper and take it slightly to the left, then immediately press down and start to bring it to the right.

2 Continue moving the brush to the right and at the end of the stroke lift it up momentarily and then press down a little.

3 Lift the brush off the paper, returning back into the stroke.

BRUSHES

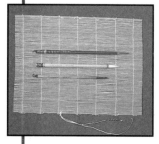

Brushes are made from different types of hair (goat, rabbit, wolf and horse) and come in a range of sizes. A good brush, which ends in a very fine tip, is highly responsive and will produce a wide range of marks. One brush, a medium-sized 'white cloud', will be enough to start with.

New brushes are protected with glue and should be soaked in warm water to remove it. When you have finished working, wash the brush well and flick it dry or shape it to a point with your fingers. Store your brushes in a pot, or hang them from the loop at the end. When carrying your brushes you should protect them in a bamboo brush holder (you can make your own from a bamboo table mat). Simply roll up the brushes inside the mat and tie with a piece of string.

GRINDING INK

The ritual of grinding the ink is all part of the preparation for your calligraphy (although you can use bottled liquid Chinese ink if you prefer). Load a little water on to the inkstone with a brush and rub the end of the ink stick in the water using circular movements. Test the ink with the brush on a piece of paper. If it spreads out rapidly along the fibres of the paper it is not ready; grind the ink stick until the colour is strong and dark. When you have finished working, wash the inkstone in warm water.

BASIC STROKES

There are eight basic strokes to master for the Standard form. Two variations of these are shown for each stroke, and the diagrams show the brush movements. Practise individual strokes before attempting a character.

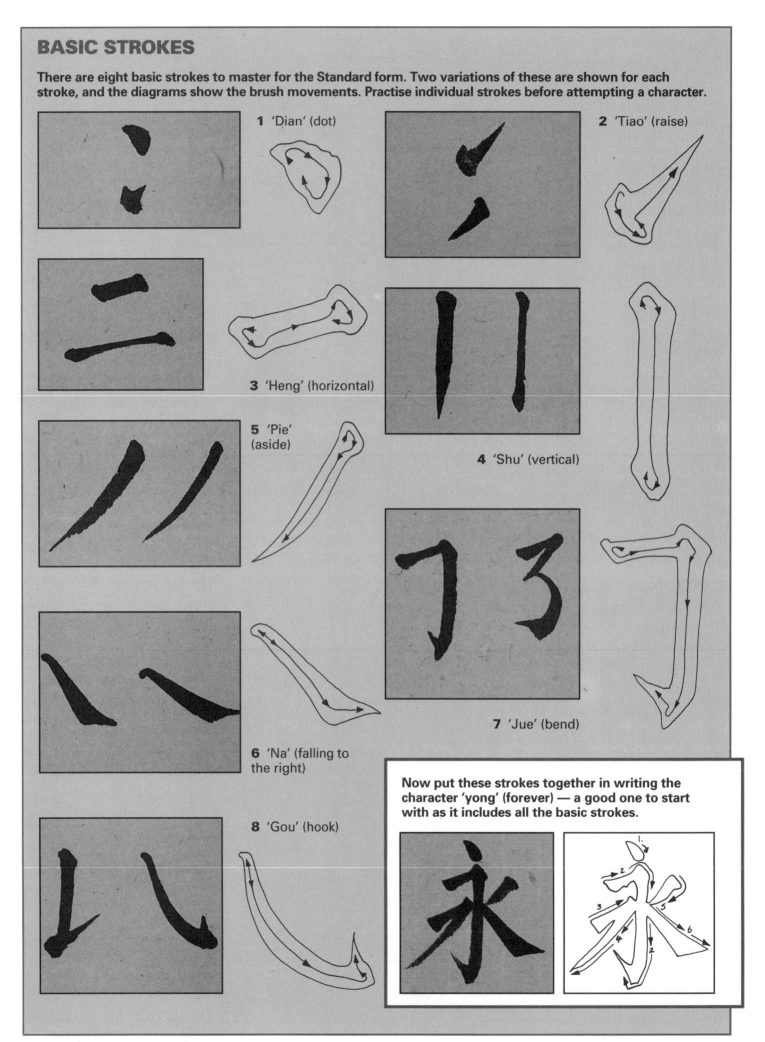

1 'Dian' (dot)

2 'Tiao' (raise)

3 'Heng' (horizontal)

4 'Shu' (vertical)

5 'Pie' (aside)

6 'Na' (falling to the right)

7 'Jue' (bend)

8 'Gou' (hook)

Now put these strokes together in writing the character 'yong' (forever) — a good one to start with as it includes all the basic strokes.

P R O J E C T

'YUN' (good luck)

1 Prepare your writing table as on page 61 and grind your ink. Dip your brush in the ink and wipe it on a tissue to shape the tip to a point. Begin to write the character 'yun' (good luck) on grass paper, copying from the example (see box) and following the order of strokes on the diagram. Some of the strokes are variations on the eight basic strokes (page 62) — stroke 1 is a dot, stroke 2 is a horizontal with a right downward hook.

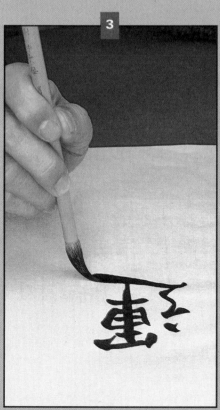

2 Stroke 3 is a horizontal, stroke 4 is a vertical, 5 is a bend (including a horizontal and a vertical); 6, 7 and 8 are horizontals. This part of the character is completed with a long vertical, 9, which ends in a sharp point.

3 The second part of the character starts with a dot, then a bend, and finishes with a long stroke falling to the right.

4 When the ink is dry, cut around the character with a pair of scissors and then cut a piece of grass paper about 3cm larger on all sides.

5 To stretch the paper, place the calligraphy face down on a piece of Conté board and dampen with water and a soft mounting brush. Dip the brush in flour and water paste (see box) and coat the paper thinly, working from the centre out to the sides.

6 Place the larger piece of paper over the calligraphy and smooth it down with the bristle mounting brush. Use a stippling action with the brush to get rid of any air bubbles.

FLOUR AND WATER PASTE

Put 3 teaspoons of flour in a bowl and add a little cold water. Mix to the consistency of cream cheese, then stir in water that has just boiled until the paste has the consistency of single cream. Strain the flour and water paste through a sieve into a pot to remove any lumps.

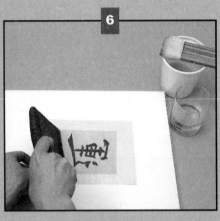

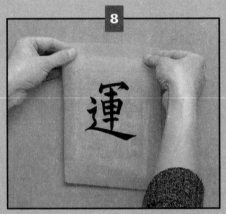

7 Brush on some more paste around the edges of the paper as shown.

8 With a palette knife, carefully lift off the paper and smooth it on to a plywood board (placed vertically) with your hands.

9 With the bristle brush, smooth the paper firmly on to the board. Add some more paste around the edges of the paper with the large soft brush, as in step 7. Leave to dry overnight.

With a knife and ruler, cut the calligraphy from the board. Fold the black card in half and stick the calligraphy to the front of the card with two small pieces of double-sided adhesive tape.

Write your message on the inside of the card with a white pencil or a gold felt-tip pen. You may wish to mount the calligraphy on a card of another colour — red or cream, for example.

CALLIGRAPHY
FAMILY TREE

MATERIALS

To make a family tree like the one shown *below left* you will need:

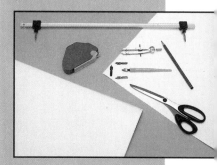

Above, white Hot Pressed watercolour paper, approximately 550 x 390mm; layout paper; pen holder; Rexel/Mitchell nibs Nos. 1¹/₂, 3¹/₂, 5 and 6; reservoir; 2H pencil; ruler; dividers; beam compasses; scissors; adhesive cassette or stick glue.

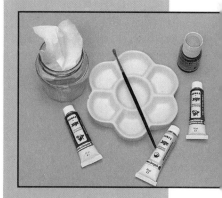

Above, gouache paints: burnt sienna, ultramarine, lemon yellow; black Indian ink; brush; jam jar; palette; tissue.

In this project we show you how to use your calligraphic skills to draw up a family tree designed as a decorative and informative panel. This would make a wonderful gift to commemorate an anniversary or a birth, or you could make one as a keepsake for your own family.

Finding out about our ancestors is becoming an increasingly popular occupation, and the research involved in putting together a family tree can uncover some fascinating facts. Once you start delving into distant history you will have to consult official records, but information about recent generations can generally be tracked down fairly easily by questioning your relations.

A family tree is a fairly complex piece of design, so it is a good idea to restrict yourself to four generations to begin with. The various elements of the design should be arranged so that they give the correct information clearly, and also create a pleasing, balanced composition. Careful planning at paste-up stage is essential. We have used an adhesive cassette to glue the pieces of paste-up, which is a very useful new product, but any glue which allows you to re-position paper can be used.

Lettering on a small scale
In this project we have also used some very small-size writing. If you are not accustomed to writing with a small nib it is advisable to work down to it gradually. Write a few lines with a size you feel comfortable with and then move down to the next size, remembering to alter your guidelines for the new nib. Practise this size until you are happy with it, then go down to the next size.

Family trees are traditionally set out with the oldest generation at the top. We have reversed this for our tree design. We have also simplified the tree, showing only one set of grandparents, and only one set of great grandparents.

HELPFUL HINT

In this project we have used two styles of writing which you will have already learnt if you have been following all the calligraphy lessons. Italic is shown on page 14. The foundational capitals are shown on pages 10-11, and their basic geometry is explained on page 28.

P R O J E C T

1 Gather together all your information and write it out roughly in your own handwriting, using the diagram *right* as guidance for the general arrangement. Rule up lines on layout paper and, working on a sloping surface, write out all the names and dates as a list without worrying about layout. The sizes we have used are given in the box *below right*, but you may want to try different writing styles and sizes.

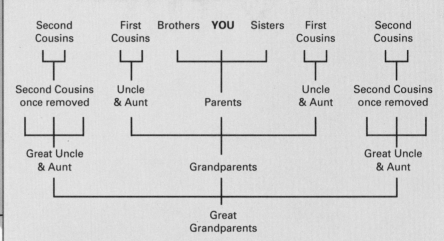

Second Cousins	First Cousins	Brothers	**YOU**	Sisters	First Cousins	Second Cousins
Second Cousins once removed	Uncle & Aunt		Parents		Uncle & Aunt	Second Cousins once removed
Great Uncle & Aunt			Grandparents			Great Uncle & Aunt

Great Grandparents

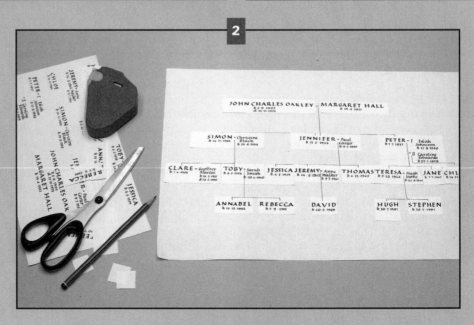

WRITING SIZES

The scripts and sizes for our family tree are given below:

Blood descendants of great grandparents: Foundational capitals with a No. 3$\frac{1}{2}$ nib at a height of 5 nib widths.

Dates and names of wives and husbands: Italics with a No. 5 nib at an x-height of 4$\frac{1}{2}$ nib widths. The space between the lines is the same as the x-height, so ascenders and descenders need to be kept short.

Heading: Foundational capitals with a No. 1$\frac{1}{2}$ nib at a height of 6 nib widths.

Family history: Italic with a No. 6 nib at a height of 4 nib widths and 3 nib widths between the lines.

Key: Foundational capitals with a No. 6 nib at a height of 4 nib widths.

2 Photocopy the names once or twice so that you can try out different layouts. Cut out the names with scissors and work out your layout. First we tried a traditional arrangement, with the oldest generation at the top and the subsequent generations arranged in lines below, with lines connecting the parents and children. The generation with the most names will determine the width of the piece (if you do not have room to put the husbands and wives on the same line, they can be placed below, preceded by the letter 'm' for married, instead of the = sign). Measure the space between the generations and then adjust by eye to make them equal.

3 In the final layout the order is reversed, with the oldest generation at the bottom of the paper. It is arranged using a simplified design of a tree as a basis for the layout, taking the idea of a family tree in a more literal way.

4 Leaving space for the foliage at the top, write the heading with widely spaced letters in a curve around the top of the design. This can be done roughly at this stage, or you can mark guidelines with the compasses as in steps 6-7. With a pencil, draw in the roots (to suggest previous generations), the trunk and the branches that indicate the lines of descent. Try to make the branches look as if they are actually growing. Draw in the foliage to group brothers and sisters together and to create a balanced design.

5 Put another sheet of layout paper over the design and mark out the areas on either side of the trunk. Rule up lines for writing in this space (see **Family history** in Writing sizes box *opposite*) and write out some details of family history. Cut out these pieces of text and stick them in position on your paste-up.

6 When all the components are organised and you are happy with your design you can prepare for your finished piece. Rule a faint vertical line centrally on a piece of Hot Pressed watercolour paper. Using beam compasses or compasses with an extension arm, draw an arc for the baseline of the heading.

7 Set the compasses for the top of the letter and rule a second arc. Take measurements from your layout for ruling lines for the names, and mark them on to a paper measurement rule (here the space between the blocks of names is 4cm on average, with slight adjustments made to accommodate ascenders and descenders). Line up the paper rule

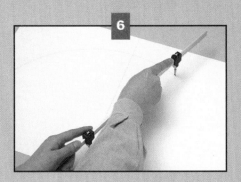

with the left side of the paper and tick off the marks as shown. Tick off the marks on the central vertical rule and, with a pencil, lightly rule all the writing lines.

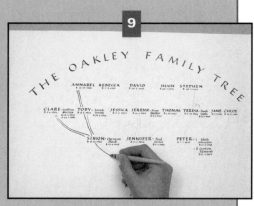

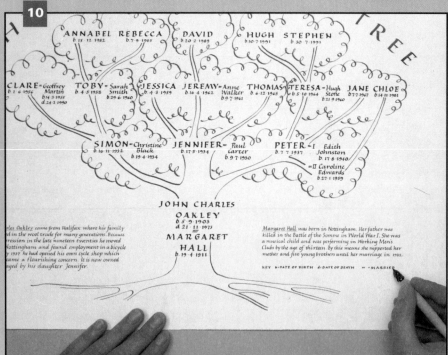

8 Using burnt sienna gouache, write the heading. The vertical strokes of letters written on a curve should point to the centre of the circle. Move the paper around as you work, so that the writing line is always horizontal to you. If you have a long family name, or need more words in the heading, you may need to use a smaller nib (remember to adjust your ruling and letter height accordingly).

9 Using your layout as a guide, write out all the names in black ink. When the ink is dry you can draw in the tree lightly with pencil, following the design on the paste-up. With burnt sienna gouache, draw the branches and tree trunk using a No. 5 nib, keeping the pen at a constant angle so that the thick and thin lines harmonise with the writing.

10 Mix ultramarine and lemon yellow to make green, and draw in the foliage using a No. 5 nib. Write the family history text with burnt sienna gouache, and the key with ink (see Writing sizes box on page 66).

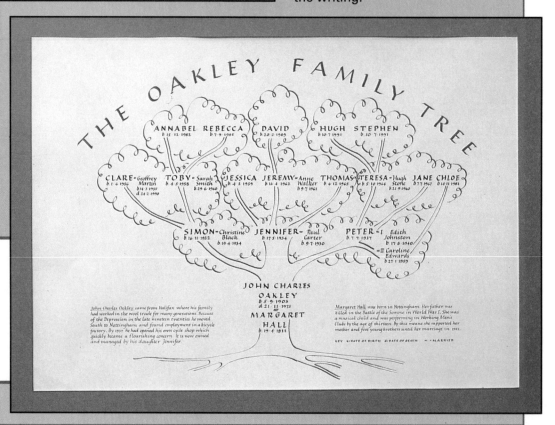

Your family tree is now ready to be mounted and framed for display. Choose colours for the mount and frame that will harmonise with the colour scheme of the family tree.

CALLIGRAPHY

HERALDRY

MATERIALS

To paint the heraldic achievement shown *below left* you will need:

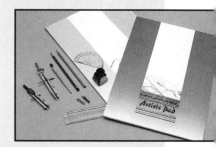

Above, A3 layout paper; A3 cartridge paper; 2H and 4B pencils; long ruler; dividers; compasses; protractor; pen holder; Mitchell/Rexell nibs, no 3, 3¹/₂, 5; non-waterproof black ink.

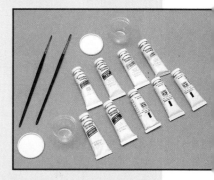

Above, gouache paints, ultramarine, cobalt, white, cadmium red, havannah lake, cadmium yellow, yellow ochre, black, lemon yellow; sable paintbrushes, sizes 1, 3; 6 miniature jam jars and lids (or other small sealable containers).

A calligrapher is often called upon to incorporate heraldic insignia in a roll of honour or diploma, and some knowledge of heraldry is essential for this. In this lesson we introduce you to the basic rules and language of heraldry, and show you how to create your own heraldic 'achievement'.

Heraldry is believed to have originated in the Middle Ages, when knights in full armour taking part in tournaments could only be identified by the colourful devices on their shield, helmet and surcoat. From the mid 12th century these 'armorial bearings' started to be passed down the family from one generation to the next, and also to be used on seals, which were important means of identification in an age when few people could read.

We tend to think of heraldry in connection with royalty and the aristocracy, but from the 14th century onwards corporations and rich merchants could apply for a grant to 'bear arms' — and this is still the case today. Anyone can apply to the College of Heralds for a Grant of Arms and it may well be granted if the applicant is an 'upright citizen' and can afford to pay for it.

Heraldry is very much a part of the modern world. In any city street you can see examples of heraldic devices on schools, colleges, civic buildings, buses, delivery vans and public house signs. Although knights no longer go into battle, 'bearing arms' is an honour much prized by, among others, city corporations and ancient seats of learning.

In this lesson we show you how to design and paint your own heraldic achievement, or armorial bearings (the shield and all its surrounding parts) and how to write out the blazon (the written description of the achievement) in proper heraldic language. We follow the rules laid down by the College of Heralds, which is the body that controls heraldry in England and Wales. Of course your own design is for fun only and should not be used in any official way.

The coats of arms of the Oxford colleges Corpus Christi, *top,* and Trinity, *above.*

THE LANGUAGE OF HERALDRY

Heraldry is a code with its own language, much of it derived from the Norman-French and Latin of the Middle Ages. At first glance it may seem complicated, but it is the most exact and concise way of talking about aspects of heraldry. On this and the following two pages we show you some of the essential elements of the heraldic code.

THE ACHIEVEMENT OF ARMS

Also referred to as the armorial bearings, this comprises the shield and all its surrounding parts. The term 'coat of arms' describes only the shield; it does not refer to the whole achievement, although it is frequently misused in this way. Dexter (right) and sinister (left) refer to the right and left of the person carrying the shield, so to onlookers, dexter is on the left and sinister on the right.

crest — wreath — mantling — helmet — shield — supporter — supporter — motto/scroll — compartment — dexter — sinister

WHILE THERE IS LIFE THERE IS HOPE

TINCTURES

Heraldic colours are called 'tinctures' and are governed by a strict code. In British heraldry there are two 'metals' (or and argent), five 'colours' (gules, azure, sable, vert and purpure) and nine 'furs' (ermine, illustrated below, is the most common). A coloured charge (symbol or device) is always placed on a metal field (background) and vice versa. Furs are exempt from this rule. If a part of the achievement is termed 'proper' it means that it is painted in natural colours.

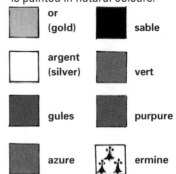

or (gold) — sable — argent (silver) — vert — gules — purpure — azure — ermine

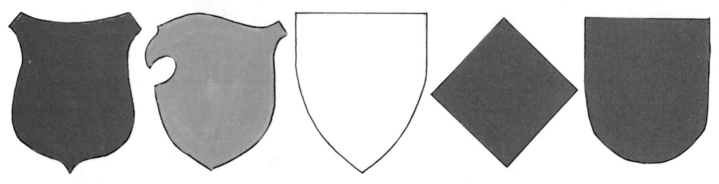

THE SHIELD

The shield is sometimes called the 'coat of arms' because in medieval times its design was embroidered on a coat worn over armour. The shield can be shown vertical or at an angle as it might have hung from a peg when not in use. It can be a variety of shapes, of which we show just a few *above*. The shield in our project is called a 'heater' because it is the shape of an iron. The lozenge shape (green, *above*) is used by single women.

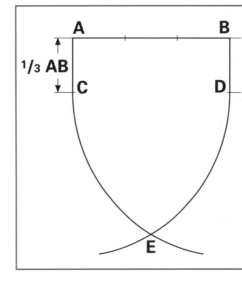

A   B
¹/₃ AB
C   D

E

DRAWING A 'HEATER' SHIELD

You will need a ruler, pencil and pair of compasses to construct the shape of the shield for the project. Start by drawing the line at the top (A-B), and then dividing it into three equal parts. Draw perpendicular lines from A and B, equal in length to one part of line A-B. Set the compasses to a radius equal to A-B. Place the point at C and draw D-E; place the point at D and draw C-E. Once you have drawn the shield it is a good idea to cut the shape from card and use it as a template when planning the work.

THE LANGUAGE OF HERALDRY

MIXING THE COLOURS FOR THE PROJECT

The colours used in heraldry should be strong and bright. Mix the paints thickly to the consistency of thin cream (see page 32). Suggestions for the colour mixes are:

Or (gold) — cadmium or Persian yellow mixed with white and yellow ochre
Argent (silver) — usually shown as white, but pale grey can be used
Gules (red) — cadmium red or vermilion or flame red
Azure (blue) — cobalt blue mixed with ultramarine and white
Sable (black) — use black gouache, not ink
Vert (green) — lemon yellow mixed with a touch of ultramarine
Purpure (purple) — light purple with a little white
Ermine — black on white

NUMBERING OF A QUARTERED SHIELD

When there are only two colours the first and fourth sections are always the same colour.

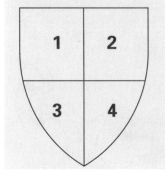

PARTED FIELDS

The surface of the shield is called the field. This can be of one colour or it can be divided, when it is called a parted field. The main ways of parting a field are: **a** per fess, **b** per pale, **c** per bend, **d** per chevron, **e** quarterly, or per cross (our project shield is parted in this way), **f** per bend sinister, **g** per saltire, **h** tierced, or per pall.

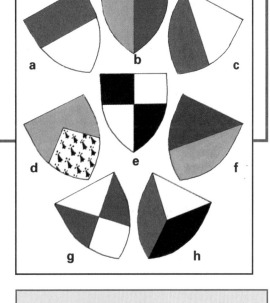

CHARGES

Symbols or emblems on the field of a shield are known as charges. Common charges are lions, fleur-de-lis, stylised roses, roundels (discs) and martlets (little birds without legs), but almost anything can be used as a charge. If the charges (or the emblems on the crest, which are often the same) refer to the bearer's name, these are said to be 'canting arms'. Shakespeare's shield bore a spear; on the shield of the City of Oxford there is an ox crossing water; in our project, windmills refer to the name (and, originally, the occupation) of the Miller family. You could choose anything appropriate to your name or occupation.

THE HELMET

Different styles of helmet, or helm, are used for different ranks. A gentleman's or esquire's helmet, **a**, has been used in the project; it is a closed helmet made of steel which always faces to the left (as you look at it). A baronet's or knight's helmet, **b**, is of steel, often with gold decoration; it has an open visor and faces front. A peer's helmet, **c**, is guarded by grilles (bars) of gold, but the helmet itself is silver and in profile. A royal helmet, **d**, faces front (affronté); it is gold and also has grilles. Paint helmets with sharply contrasting highlights and shadows to give a shiny metallic appearance. The inside is usually painted dark red to suggest a velvet lining.

THE WREATH

Also known as the torse, in medieval times this was a circle of silk with gold and silver thread twisted around it, covering the join between the crest and the helmet. It is always shown as six alternate twists, usually of the principal colour and metal, beginning on the left with the metal.

THE CREST

In battle the crest was worn on top of the helmet as a further mark of identification, and so is often similar to the main charge. In our project the crest is a windmill similar to the charges on the shield, but depicted in a more three-dimensional way.

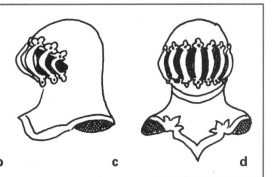

THE LANGUAGE OF HERALDRY

MANTLING

This was originally a cloth cape worn to protect the back of the neck from the heat of the sun. Nowadays it appears as stylised torn fabric or foliage. Its colour should be the principal colour of the shield with a lining of the principal metal. The lining and top fabric should appear equally visible. It is usually shaded and the light source is assumed to come from the top left.

Right: **The armorial bearings of Lord North shows an unconventional interpretation of the heraldic rules, but is still 'correct' in its form. The blazon is written in capital letters in a border around the achievement, making it an integral part of the design.**

MOTTO AND SCROLL

The motto is written on a scroll of white cloth, which can be arranged in various ways. Drawing the scroll with double pencils (see page 25) may help you make the folds look convincing. The words of the motto are often in Latin, and some mottoes incorporate a pun on the name. For instance, the motto of the Fortescue family is '*Forte scutum salus ducum*' meaning 'a strong shield is the leader's safeguard'; the Seton family use the motto 'Set on'.

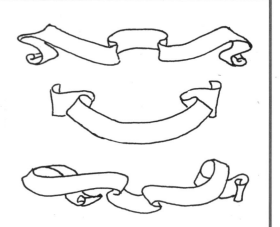

THE SUPPORTERS

Supporters are a great honour and are only granted officially to individuals on rare occasions, but there is no reason why they should not be included in an achievement designed for fun. Many countries, cities and city companies have them. They can be animals or humans or mythical creatures; they can both be the same or two different species. Australia has, appropriately, a kangaroo and an emu; the city of London has two dragons, the Swedish polar explorer Baron Adolf Erik Nordenskiöld had two polar bears and the Royal Arms of the United Kingdom are supported by a lion and a unicorn. The Miller family achievement has a cat and a dog for supporters, which are based on ancient designs. Supporters should appear imposing, if not somewhat fierce, as they are the guardians of the shield.

THE COMPARTMENT

The supporters need somewhere to stand to emphasise their stability. This is usually depicted, as in our project, as a stylised grassy mound, but it could be pebbles, a sandy shore, or even a brick wall.

THE BLAZON

The blazon is a written description in heraldic language of the whole achievement. It provides the heraldic artist with all the information needed to paint the achievement. At first it may seem difficult to understand but it is in fact an exact and very precise description. The blazon can be written in any style of lettering, but it should complement the design and style of the achievement. The blazon of the Miller family is given below. The information on these pages will help you understand most of the words, but a full explanation is given to help you write a blazon for your own achievement.

The Miller family blazon

Shield	— Quarterly or and azure. First and fourth a windmill gules.
Crest	— Upon a wreath of the colours a windmill gules.
Supporters	— On the dexter side, a dog, on the sinister side a cat proper.
Motto	— While there is life there is hope.

Shield — 'Quarterly or and azure' means that the field is divided in four. Or (gold), being the first colour mentioned, is in the first and fourth sections; azure (blue) is in the second and third sections. 'First and fourth a windmill gules' describes the charges (windmills), their position (first and fourth sections), and their colour (gules, or red).
Crest — 'A wreath of the colours' means the two main colours (or and azure); it is not always in the main colours. The mantling is not mentioned because it is always in the two main colours.
Supporters — 'On the dexter side a dog' means the dog appears to us on the left. 'Proper' means the supporters are painted in natural colours, rather than heraldic tinctures. The compartment is only mentioned if it is not a plain grassy mound.

PROJECT

ARMORIAL BEARINGS

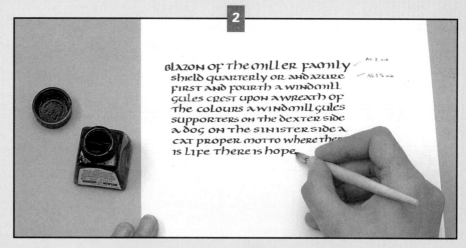

1 Do a rough drawing of the achievement in pencil, referring to the information on the previous pages. You may like to copy ours before you compose your own so that you are familiar with the technique and so will be better prepared to anticipate design

problems. Construct the shield first (see page 70), and draw the rest of the components, making sure that the design is balanced and in proportion. Write the blazon in your own handwriting below, to get the general scheme of the layout arranged.

2 On layout paper, mark out the area for the text, and select a nib and writing size that works within the space. Write out the text. We used uncial letterforms (see page 23); a no 3 nib for the heading, and a 3¹/₂ nib for the text.

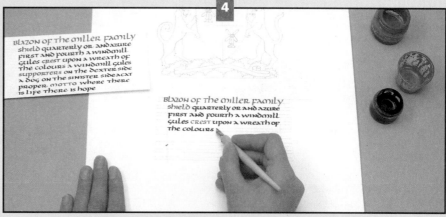

3 Transfer the outline of the achievement to cartridge paper (rub pencil on the back of the outline and trace over the line on the right side with a pencil).

4 Go over the outline of the achievement with pencil to tidy up the details. Rule the lines for the writing, using dividers to mark out the lines. Write the main heading in blue, the other headings in red and use black gouache to write the rest of the text.

5 Protect the written area of the work with a piece of paper. Paint the large flat areas of colour with the no 3 sable brush, working quickly and keeping the surface of the paint smooth. Wash the brush

HELPFUL HINT

Mix up generous quantities of the colours in small jam jars, or other containers with airtight lids, so that they can be stored and reused (see page 71 for mixing the colours: azure, gules, or and sable).

well before changing colours. The first and fourth sections of the shield and the lining of the mantling are or; the second and third sections and the top fabric of the mantling are azure. Paint the steel helmet with a mid-grey (achieved by mixing black and white with a touch of ultramarine); the lining of the helmet is painted with havannah lake to give a dark red. The windmills are gules.

6 Mix the colours for the modelling to give the appearance of light and shade and paint the tones with the no 1 sable brush. The windmill on the crest is modelled with havannah lake. Paint the highlights on the helmet with white paint and paint the shadows with some of the grey added to black. For the lining of the mantling, mix a lighter tone of or by adding a little white to part of the colour; mix a darker tone by adding more cadmium yellow and a touch of cadmium red. The azure mantling is lightened with white, and darkened with ultramarine.

7 Paint a flat area of yellow ochre over the whole of the bodies of the supporters (the cat and dog). Model the cat with a light and mid-grey and then with black, using small brushstrokes to imitate fur. Model the dog with black. Paint white fur on the cat and the dog; paint the tongues red, the eyes green. Paint the compartment (the grassy mound) with a mix of lemon yellow and a touch of ultramarine over the whole area. The zig-zag tufts of grass are painted with the green darkened with more ultramarine. The scroll is shaded largely with water, darkened with a tiny touch of ink.

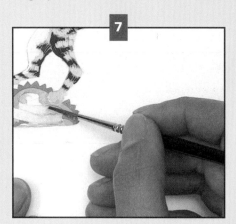

8 When the scroll is dry, pencil in the motto lightly, then write it in small foundational capital letters with a no 5 nib using black gouache.

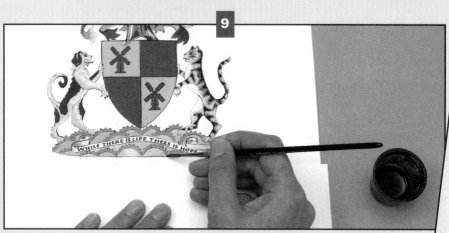

9 Mix havannah lake with black and paint a fine outline around the whole design, making sure that the no 1 brush is brought to a fine point. Darken the markings of the cat's body.

When you have finished your achievement you can frame it and display it in your hall or living room. It would make an original gift to mark a birth or other family occasion.

BLAZON OF THE MILLER FAMILY
shield quarterly or and azure
FIRST AND FOURTH A WINDMILL
gules crest upon a wreath of
the colours a windmill gules
SUPPORTERS on the dexter side
a dog on the sinister side a
cat proper motto where there
is life there is hope

CALLIGRAPHY

DECORATIVE MAP

In this calligraphy lesson, you will have the opportunity to use several hands that you have learnt in previous lessons and to discover the art of flourishing. Our project shows you how to make a decorative map, and how to make use of a photocopier in the preparation of the design.

When designing a map you can bring many aspects of calligraphy into play. The first consideration is the function of the piece, and of making a cohesive design of the many elements. You have the opportunity to combine calligraphy with illustration. You will have different types of information to convey in writing. This can be done by restricting yourself to one script written at different sizes and weights, or by using several different scripts for different types of information. And a decorative map is an ideal place to consider adding a flourish to your work. In this project we have used flourishes for the name of the village and as part of a monogram device (see page 48) which forms part of the design.

Our map is designed to be incorporated into an address card, and reproduced on a photocopier. Since it is on a fairly small scale it is easier to work on a larger scale and to reduce it on a photocopier for reproduction. Reducing the work also tends to improve the appearance of the writing (although too much reduction will tend to distort it). You can use a paste-up to copy from.

The design process is just the same for a wall display map, but you might want to consider colour as a part of the design throughout, and after arranging the design as a paste-up the last stage would be to write it on a good-quality piece of paper. For a more ambitious project, you could embellish the map with poems and texts which have historical or literary associations with the area.

MATERIALS

To make the calligraphic map shown *below left* you will need:

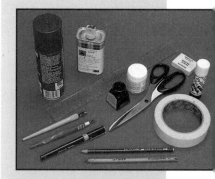

Above, non-waterproof ink; pen holder; Mitchell/Rexel nibs, nos 2, 3, 3½ and 4; reservoir; mapping pen; technical drawing pen; pencil; red coloured pencil; masking tape; scissors; stick glue; eraser; ruler; white-out paint; spray glue and lighter fuel.

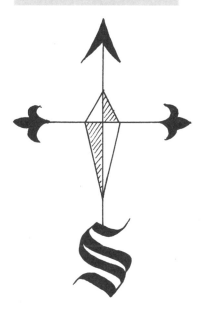

Above, A3 layout pad; sheet of tracing paper; selection of papers for copying and matching envelopes.

MAP DESIGN

Before embarking on your map it is important to be clear about the function it will perform, and to consider whether it needs to be accurately to scale. If it is a map to be reproduced, this will affect the way that you prepare it. If it is going to be photocopied or printed it can be prepared in black and white as a paste-up, which will save time (you can print from colour artwork, but this can be expensive).

ROUGH DESIGNS

Start by making rough thumbnail sketches of the whole map, considering what you are going to include and what you will leave out. The plan can be drawn from memory or, for greater accuracy of scale, you can refer to street maps. Think about the general design and the format of the piece.

SYMBOLS

Invent symbols and simplified illustrations to represent various features on the map, considering the style of drawing. Drawings that are made with an edged pen will naturally work well as they will relate to the line of the writing. However, you might like to try other tools such as a pencil or brush. These examples show some of the symbols that we considered for the project.

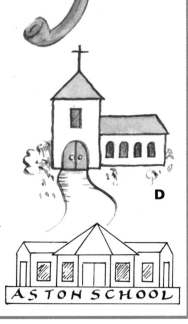

A Water and grass are represented by marks made with the broad-edged pen. The thin strokes of the tufts of grass are made by turning the pen to a very steep angle.

B Use a mapping pen to draw features such as trees, exaggerating the characteristics of their shape to make them easy to identify.

C Industrial buildings, such as the sawmill, and features such as telephone boxes can be represented by symbols of the trade.

D Simplify the shape of buildings. Outlines can be drawn with a thin-edged pen or, for a thin, even line use a technical drawing pen or a fine monoline fibre-tipped pen.

LETTER FORMS

A map design gives the opportunity of using several different scripts together. Experiment with the scripts you have learnt in previous lessons to write different types of information. Keep to simple, appropriate letter forms for the majority of the text, but give a more elaborate treatment to the name of the town or village. Remember that a map must be clear, so avoid a cluttered design with too much variety.

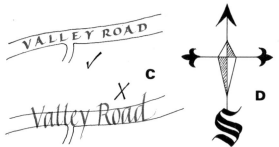

A Foundational hand (see page 10) is a clear and useful hand for maps.

B Uncials (see page 23) are also strong and highly legible, but are slightly more decorative.

C Widely spaced capital letters are suitable for road names as they fit comfortably between the lines and there is no problem with ascenders and descenders.

D An ornate gothic letter on the arrow of the compass makes good use of this highly decorative script.

FLOURISHES

Flourishes are curved, natural-looking extensions to the strokes of letters that can add a decorative touch to the writing.

Italic and foundational capital letters lend themselves readily to flourishing, as do the ascenders and descenders of lower case italic.

On this page we show you a 'swash' capital alphabet, where you can see flourishes beginning to grow from the letters. Practise these letters before moving on to the more ambitious flourishes — the aim is to make the flourishes flow smoothly from the letter. Flourishing is not easy, so practise until your confidence with the pen grows.

FLOURISHING

For complex flourishes it can be helpful to first draw in the lines of the flourish in pencil so that you have a rough guide. Follow the order of strokes for the letters *below*, then design your own flourishes for other letters, based on the alphabet on this page.

SWASH CAPITAL ALPHABET

FLOURISHES IN CONTEXT

Allow plenty of space around flourishes within a piece of writing. Minimal flourishes work well at the beginning and end of lines of writing (and note that the foot of the lower case 'd' in the address has also been given a small flourish). Flourishes must be made to balance within the design of a word or a piece of writing. In the word ASTON, the balance has a diagonal stress.

FREE FLOURISHES

Once you have understood the idea of flourishing, and the shapes you are trying to achieve, you could try writing them freely in one movement. You will need a bold approach, a sweeping arm movement and a light touch. Some of the lines may disappear altogether, but that is the nature of this type of letter. This freely flourished letter 'R' was written with an automatic pen, which is particularly useful for this approach.

P R O J E C T

ADDRESS CARD

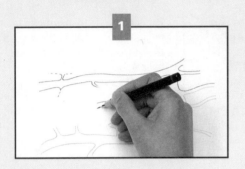

1

BEFORE YOU BEGIN

Mark out an A4 sheet of paper as shown to indicate the fold lines so that you know the final size and proportions of the design area. We will design the map at a larger size and then reduce it on a photocopier to fit.

MONOGRAM (front)	
ADDRESS (inside left)	**MAP** (inside right)

1 Draw thumbnail sketches of your map (see page 76). Draw the roads and any other major outlines on a piece of layout paper in pencil, then go over the lines with a technical pen.

2 Put a sheet of tracing paper over it and practise writing the names of the roads in pencil and then pen. Use a smaller nib to write names at a smaller size to keep the weight of the letters similar.

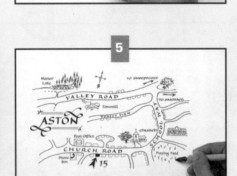

2

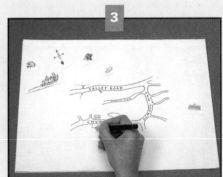

3

3 Write the road names on the map using the nos 3 and 3½ nibs. Draw the symbols on a sheet of paper and cut them out, then arrange them on the map. You can stick them down, or redraw them directly on to the map.

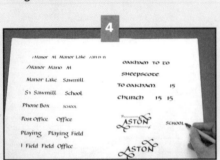

4

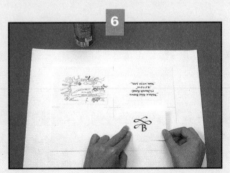

5

4 Write the wording for the features and place names at sizes that you feel comfortable with. Reduce these on a photocopier, cut out, spray the backs with glue and stick in position on the map.

5 Add any other elements and final details by hand, using a nib of appropriate size.

6 Write the name and address in italic on layout paper. We used a no 3½ nib and then reduced it by 20%. Write the monogram (we used a no 2 nib). Reduce all the elements to the correct size on a photocopier, and stick them on the sheet of A4 paper as shown. Rub out the fold marks, clean off any excess glue with lighter fuel and a tissue, and cover up any marks with white-out paint.

6

*Mike & Alice Brown
15 Church Road
ASTON
Mon NT91 3OR*

7

You can photocopy on to any type or colour of paper as long as it fits into the machine. If you have made a map card the same size as ours it will fit into a standard envelope.

7 Make as many photocopies as you need, and fold each sheet along the long fold and then the short fold. Add touches of red coloured pencil in the borders around the name.

MAKING PAPER

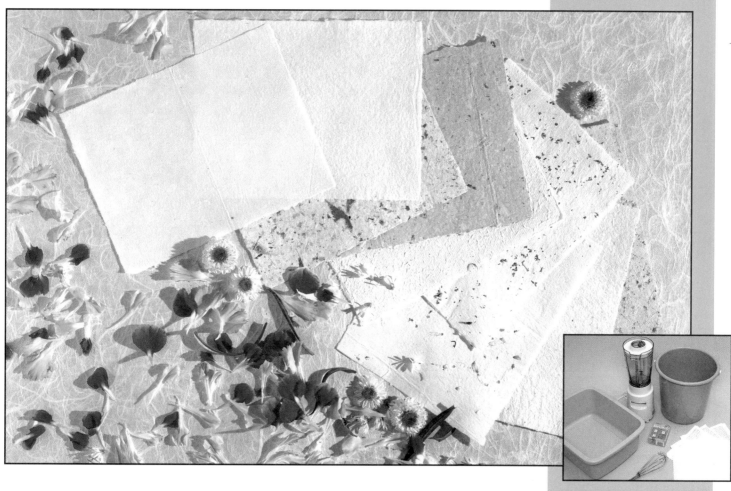

MATERIALS

To make the paper shown *below*, you will need:

Handmade paper is usually thought of as a luxury item used by fine artists and crafts people. In this project we introduce you to the art of making your own paper, using scrap paper, producing a highly desirable textured writing paper that will give your letters an air of distinction.

Paper is made up of tiny fibres, which become entangled during the production process. In machine-made paper the fibres tend to line up in one direction, which is why you can easily tear it along the grain. In handmade paper the fibres are randomly dispersed, so the paper is difficult to tear in any direction. It is this quality that gives handmade paper its superior quality.

Handmade paper is formed on a 'frame', which is made of two sections: the mould and the deckle. The mould has a fine mesh that acts like a sieve; the deckle is held in position on top of the mould to confine the fibres within the sheet area. The edge of the finished sheet of paper is always ragged, and derives its name 'deckled edge' from the deckle.

When using waste paper, the type of paper you choose will make a considerable difference to the quality of the finished product. Use paper with a matt finish rather than a glossy one, as glossy paper is coated with varnishes and other products that prevent the fibres breaking down.

The whiter the original paper, the better your handmade paper will be. A cheap, printed paper containing a high amount of ink, such as newspaper, will give a weak, greyish hand result. You can reduce the discoloration of paper made from newsprint by adding two to three teaspoonfuls of bleach to a bucket of pulp. Pour the pulp into a preserving saucepan and boil for a few minutes, removing the scum from the surface as it appears. If you want to produce coloured paper, add a cold-water dye to the pulp.

Above, waste paper; square washing-up bowl; plastic bucket; liquidiser, 1L capacity; balloon whisk; gelatine.

Above, all-purpose cloths; palette knife. If you want to press your paper (see page 84) you will need the following: two flat wooden boards, 240 x 300 x 18mm; four G-clamps; 12 pieces of felt, 230 x 280mm; sheets of newsprint or newspaper; rolling pin.

MATERIALS

4 pieces of hardwood, 220 x 20 x 20mm
4 pieces of hardwood, 210 x 20 x 20mm
piece of car repair mesh, or fabric
mesh (such as curtain netting) with
10-15 holes per sq cm
frame clamp
8 brass angle irons
16 brass screws (supplied with the
angle irons)
bradawl
screwdriver
glass paper
brass panel pins
hammer
waterproof glue
polyurethane varnish

MAKING THE MOULD AND DECKLE

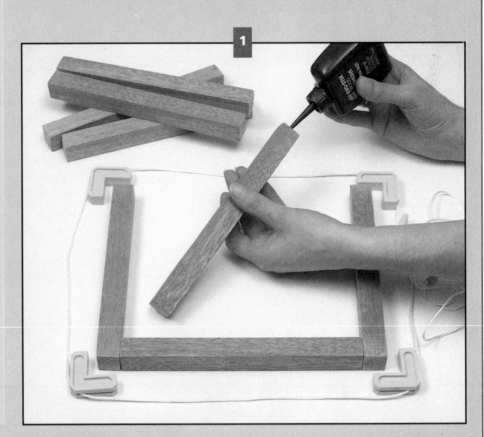

1 Sand the ends of each piece of wood until they are square. To make the mould, glue two long and two short pieces together to form a rectangle, attaching the shorter pieces to the ends of the longer pieces. Position the frame clamp around the mould and tighten the clamp to ensure that the corners of the mould remain square. Leave to dry. Remove the frame clamp when the glue has dried. Repeat with the other four pieces of wood to make the deckle.

2 Position an angle iron at one of the corners of the mould. Use the bradawl to make holes through the the outermost screw holes and into the wood. Insert the screws and repeat for the other three corners. Varnish the frame and, while it is drying, complete the deckle in the same way.

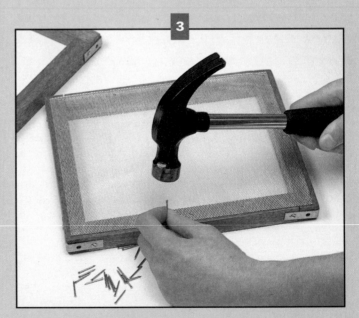

3 Place the mesh on one side of the mould and attach it with panel pins along all four sides, making certain the mesh is taut.

P R O J E C T

1 Rip the waste paper into pieces approximately 3cm square. Place the paper in a bucket of cold water and leave it to soak overnight to break down the fibres. If you want to speed up this process, use boiling water instead of cold water and let the paper soak for a few hours.

2 Put some of the paper into the liquidiser and reduce it to a pulp. The thickness of the paper you make will be determined by the ratio of water to paper that you use in pulping. To begin with, use 10-15 pieces of paper to ¾L of water. You can alter the ratio when you become familiar with the process. Liquidise the pulp for approximately 10 seconds; it should have a creamy consistency. If any large pieces remain, liquidise for a few more seconds.

3 Pour the pulp into a square washing-up bowl, filling it three-quarters full.

4 Place the deckle on top of the mould. Agitate the pulp with a balloon whisk.

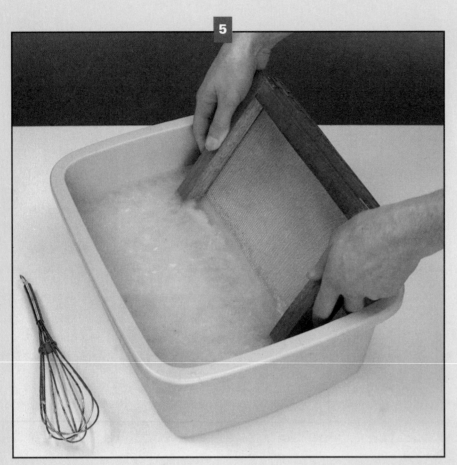

5 Hold the mould and deckle together to make a 'frame', and insert the frame into the pulp at an angle as shown.

SIZING

You can write on your handmade paper with a pencil or ballpoint pen, but the ink from a fountain pen will 'bleed' into the paper. You can overcome this problem by sizing the paper, either during or after the papermaking process. Add half a sachet of gelatine dissolved in 150ml hot water to the pulp when it is in the bowl, or paint or spray the gelatine solution on to the paper while it is still wet.

6 When it is fully submerged, hold the frame horizontally and shake it gently — forwards and backwards and from side to side — so that the paper fibres are evenly distributed over the mesh.

7 Carefully lift the frame out of the pulp, keeping it in a horizontal position. Before removing it completely, shake the frame from side to side to prevent any ripples from forming. As you lift the frame out of the pulp the suction will draw the fibres on to the mesh.

8 Hold the frame over the bowl and tilt the frame slightly to allow the excess water to drain away.

9 Remove the deckle from the mould, taking care to avoid dripping water on to the paper pulp on the mould. A rectangular piece of paper will be left on the surface of the mould. Use one of the methods described below to dry the paper.

DRYING THE PAPER

There are three ways in which you can dry your paper.

METHOD 1
Leave the paper on the mould. When it has dried, lift it carefully from the mould with a palette knife. Drying paper on a mould produces a rough, but pleasant, finish. This method is most suitable for drying your final sheet. If you want to dry all your sheets in this way you will need more than one mould.

METHOD 2
If you only have one mould you can transfer the paper to a cloth to dry.

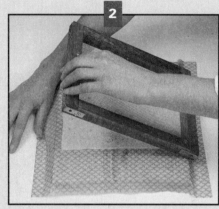

1 Dampen an all-purpose cloth and lay it out flat. Turn the mould upside-down on to the cloth and press it gently but firmly.

2 Carefully pull the mould away from the paper. If you have difficulty in separating the mould and the paper, place the cloth on a slightly curved surface, such as an upturned plate. The paper will then come away easily from the mould. Put the cloth on a flat surface and leave undisturbed until the paper has dried. Repeat for your other sheets, laying each cloth out singly; do not stack them into a pile.

METHOD 3
You can begin the drying process and at the same time achieve a smooth surface by putting your paper into a press. If you do not have access to a bookbinder's press (known as a nipping press) you can made a simple device with two pieces of board and four G-clamps. The paper is interleaved with newspaper and felt and 'sandwiched' between the boards.

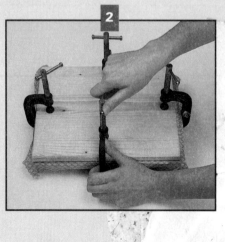

1 Put some sheets of newspaper on top of one of the boards. As you make each sheet of paper, turn it out on to a dampened all-purpose cloth, as described in Method 2. Place the cloth and paper on top of the newspaper, and lay a sheet of felt on top. Continue to stack layers of cloth, paper and felt until you have made all your paper. Then finish off with some more sheets of newspaper.

2 Place the second board on top of the pile and fit a G-clamp to the centre of each side so that the clamps hold the sandwich together loosely. Secure the clamps by tightening first one opposite pair, and then the other, so that the excess water in the paper is squeezed out. To complete the drying process, unclamp the press, remove the cloths (with the papers still lying on them) from the press and hang them up to dry indoors on a clothes line. Do not attempt to speed up the drying process as the paper will warp.

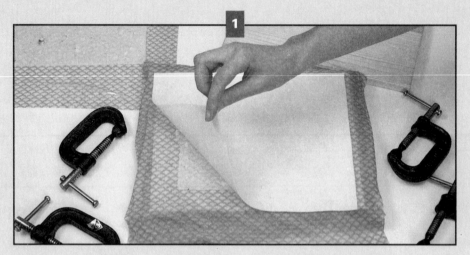

If you want your paper to have a very smooth surface, place it while still damp on a piece of glass or perspex and, using a rolling pin, carefully roll from the centre of the sheet out to the edges, taking care not to crease the paper. You can create attractively textured papers by adding vegetable material such as small flower petals, leaves or stems. Either mix them into the pulp at step 3 or sprinkle them on top of it at the end of step 4 before submerging the frame.

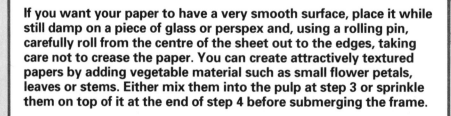

PAPERCRAFT

LEAF MOTIF PAPER

In this project we show you how to create your own watermark on vegetable-dyed writing paper and matching envelopes. We also show you a simple method of shallow embossing for a subtle additional decorative finish.

Watermarks can be seen in paper when it is held up against a light source. They are created by wire designs, symbols or words which are fixed to the mesh of the mould and so create a thinner area of paper along the lines of wire when the paper is made. Originally they denoted the papermaker's or the mill's trademark, or information about the quality or size of the sheet. Today they are sometimes used by companies for security purposes, or to add a distinguished touch to personal writing paper.

We have used a watermark based on a leaf design, but you may like to create your own design from a symbol or your initials. The watermark design is echoed in the shallow embossing at the top and bottom of the paper, which is achieved by simply rubbing around a leaf shape cut out of card.

The paper pulp is dyed green by adding leek fibres to the pulp, or you can use onion skins to give a pale yellow-brown colour. In the latter case, put 2-3 handfuls of the outer, papery onion skins in 4 litres of soft water and then bring the liquid to the boil. Simmer for one hour, then strain and proceed as at step 6 on page 87, adding a teaspoonful of turmeric and a pinch of purified cream of tartar to the water in the liquidiser to strengthen the colour.

Vegetable fibres alone produce a paper with a weak structure, which although decorative, is not suitable for writing paper. So we have strengthened our paper by adding cotton linter. The texture of the cloths used for soaking up the water while drying will determine the surface of the paper. For a smooth surface, use cloths with a smooth finish, without any holes.

MATERIALS

To make the paper and envelopes shown *below left* you will need:

Above, mould and deckle (see page 258); 60cm of 0.7mm gauge silver wire; fine (5-amp) fuse wire; half-round pliers; small piece of card; scalpel and blades; set square; pencil; glue; steel ruler; masking tape; tracing paper.

Above, waste paper; 1 sheet cotton linter; bucket; square washing-up bowl; liquidiser, 1 litre capacity; 1 sachet of gelatine; ¹/₂lb leeks; saucepan; knife; colander; muslin.

Above, mould and deckle (see page 80); 60cm of 0.7mm gauge silver wire; fine (5-amp) fuse wire; half-round pliers; small piece of card; scalpel and blades; set square; pencil; glue; steel ruler; masking tape; tracing paper.

P R O J E C T

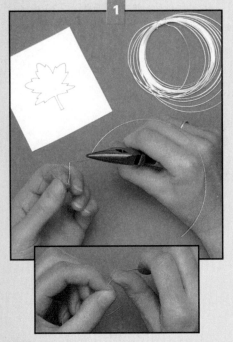

2 Add the details to the leaves by bending the wire to follow the inner (black) outline on the template. Create a second leaf shape with the other piece of wire, but do not worry if the leaves are not identical — you are representing natural forms which are all individual. The leaves will go out of shape before they are attached to the mesh.

1 Cut the silver wire into two 30cm lengths. Bend one piece of wire with the pliers to follow the main (coloured) outline on the template, curving the wire over your thumb as shown.

LEAF TEMPLATE AND DESIGN GUIDE

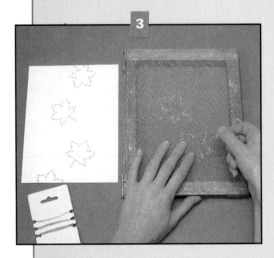

3 Enlarge the leaf template on a photocopier at 145%. Enlarge the design guide 200%, then 170%. Cut out around the margins. The two central leaves will be watermarks. Place the design guide beside or beneath the mesh of the mould and place one wire 'leaf' in position. Cut several 3cm lengths of fuse wire and fold in half. Thread one piece over the wire of the leaf and through the mesh, hold in position with one finger, turn the mould over and twist the ends to secure at the back. Secure at several points around the leaf until it lies flat. Repeat for the other leaf.

4 Trim off the ends of the fuse wire at the back using the pliers.

5 Boil the leeks for 30 minutes until mushy, then strain into a piece of muslin placed over a colander. Rinse under a tap until the water runs clear. Gather up the muslin and squeeze out the remaining water.

6 Make up the paper pulp mixture (see page 81) using 5 litres of water and about 50 pieces each of torn up waste paper and cotton linter. Pour into the bowl. Dissolve the gelatine according to the instructions and add to the pulp. Liquidise the leek fibres with some water. For a subtle green dye, liquidise for at least

15 seconds; for a stronger green, stop after a few seconds and check. Add to the paper pulp.

7 Agitate the pulp with your hand. Place the deckle on the mould and insert into the pulp at an angle. Move the frame to disperse the fibres evenly (see page 82).

HELPFUL HINT

If you wish to make some paper a subtle green and some with more pronounced green fibres, pour some of the liquidised leeks into a container after liquidising for a few seconds, and add it to the pulp after you have made a few sheets of pale green paper. As a contrast, you can colour your paper with onion skins, or make it plain white.

8 Lift the frame out of the pulp, keeping it horizontal. Remove the deckle. Tip the mould slightly to drain off remaining water (see bottom picture).

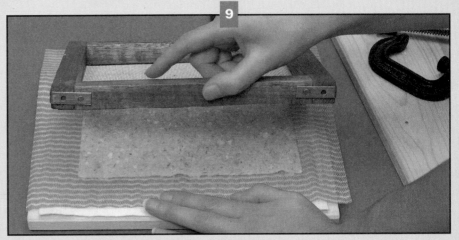

9 Stack and dry the paper (see Method 3, page 84).

10 Trace the black leaf template on to a piece of thick card and cut out the shape with a scalpel. Stick the shape (with masking tape on the back) at the top of the design guide.

HELPFUL HINT

To create a smooth surface, place the sheet of paper with its cloth on a flat, smooth surface. Roll the surface of the paper lightly with a rolling pin. Do not press too hard or you will distort the watermark.

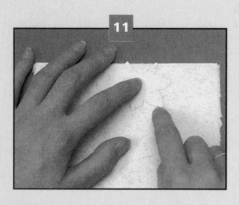

11 Place a sheet of your dried paper on the design guide and press down around the leaf outline with your finger. Then with your fingernail or the rounded end of a pencil, define the edges of the leaf to achieve a shallow, embossed impression. Be careful not to rip the paper. Repeat for the leaf at the bottom of the paper.

ENVELOPE TEMPLATE

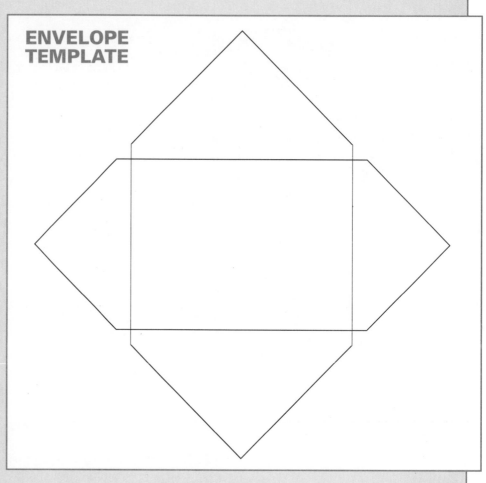

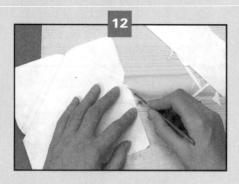

12 Photocopy the envelope template at 200% and cut around the margins. Place the template on a sheet of handmade paper and cut carefully around the outline with a very sharp scalpel. (Cut the straight lines against a ruler and then cut the rounded corners.)

HELPFUL HINT

The fibres of the paper tear very easily, so if you do not have a very sharp knife, cut out the envelope with a pair of scissors. You can leave the ragged edges of the paper if they are very near the outline.

13 Fold along the pencil lines and glue two sides as shown.

Use a felt pen to write on the paper; a hard point, such as a fountain pen, may catch in the fibres. When you want to use one of your envelopes, seal the flap with a dot of glue, or use sealing wax for a distinctive finish.

MARBLED PAPER

Oil marbling is one of the most direct techniques employed to make decorated papers. The reaction of oil colour and water in its simplest form provides a fascinating medium for achieving original decorative results.

MATERIALS

To make the marbled papers shown *below left* you will need:

Above, small plastic bucket; plastic tray, approximately 30 x 37cm; cellulose wallpaper paste; wooden spoon or mixing stick; sheets of A4 paper, such as typing or photocopy paper; newsprint or newspaper, to protect your work surface.

The history of marbled papers has long been associated with Asia, especially the Far East. The earliest examples of decorative marbling can be traced back to the Japanese, who were making use of them as early as the 8th century. Subtly marked marbled papers, known as suminagashi, were used for calligraphy. The paper was partially marbled in selected areas, perhaps as an early form of authenticating documents.

Extensive use of marbling was made in Persia and Turkey around the 16th century, notably as part of the integral design and decoration on miniature paintings and illuminated manuscripts. With the advent of merchants operating actively in the Middle East and Asia, sheets of marbled paper became increasingly available. At this time they were used mainly to line the interiors of boxes, bound eventually for the European market, and subsequently the art of marbling reached the western world. More recently, marbled papers have been associated with the art of bookbinding, and are the classic medium for decorated endpapers. Today marbling is applied to a broader field, taking in packaging and gift wrap as well as pure decorative art.

The traditional method of marbling paper relies on the process of floating watercolour (mixed with ox gall, which acts as a floating agent) on the surface of a thickened size made of Irish moss (carragheen moss). Here we have replaced watercolours with student quality oil paints. The size is made from a cellulose wallpaper paste to provide a more direct process for making handmade marbled papers.

Although you will find that the marbling takes very little time, you will have to allow about 24 hours for your prints to dry. Once they are thoroughly dry you can, if you wish, place them under several heavy books to press them flat.

Above, student's oil paints in blue, red, yellow, black and green; four glass jars; white spirit; three paint brushes, size 6; four glass droppers or pipettes.

P R O J E C T

1 For the base liquid, or 'bath', mix up the wallpaper paste and water in a small plastic bucket, following the manufacturer's directions and adding more water if necessary until the mixture is the consistency of single cream. Stir all the time as you mix to make certain the paste is kept free of lumps.

2 Cover your work surface with newsprint or newspaper and mix the oil colour by squeezing out 20mm of paint into a clean glass jar. Using a dropper or pipette, add a few drops of white spirit and stir with a paint brush until the paint has dissolved. Continue to add white spirit until the mixture is thin enough to be drawn up into the dropper. Mix three or four other colours in the same way.

3 Transfer your base liquid to a plastic tray, filling the tray to a minimum depth of 5cm. Arrange the jars of paint, paper for marbling and droppers close to the tray of paste.

4 Draw up some blue colour into the dropper and drop a few spots on to the surface of the bath. Rock the tray to and fro a few times to allow the paint to disperse a little. Add a few more drops of colour and swirl the paint with a paint brush.

5 When the colour has spread evenly on the surface, add a few drops of red colour. Gently swirl again with a paint brush, then allow the paint to spread and settle for a few seconds.

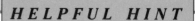

HELPFUL HINT

If the paint sinks to the bottom of the tray after it has been dropped on to the surface of the base liquid it is too thick, and you will have to dilute it further with white spirit. If, however, you have diluted it too much the paint will disperse too quickly on the surface and you will have to add more paint to the diluted solution.

6 Gently lay your first piece of paper on the water by dropping one of the corners on to the surface of the bath and then releasing the paper to float on the surface.

HELPFUL HINT

When you place your paper on the bath, make certain there are no air bubbles trapped underneath the paper; if there are, gently tap the bubbles from the back of the paper to release the air. If the air bubbles are left they will create white areas on the marbling.

7 Leave the paper in the bath for a few seconds, then remove it carefully by two corners. Lay the paper out on a piece of newspaper and leave to dry for about 24 hours.

8 To achieve a mottled effect, rather than the more traditional marbled one, let a few drops of black disperse on the surface of the bath and leave for one minute. If you wish, you can rock the tray a little to help the colour disperse.

CHANGING COLOURS

If you want to print with different colours, you will need to clear the surface of the bath of existing colour. To do this, lay a piece of newsprint or newspaper — cut to the size of the bath — on top of the bath, and repeat two to three times with fresh paper until all the excess paint has been removed. The bath can be cleaned in this way time after time.

9 Using a small brush, delicately spot a second colour on to the surface, then add a third colour. A number of colours can be used in this way; some will merge to give extra colours to enrich the marbling.

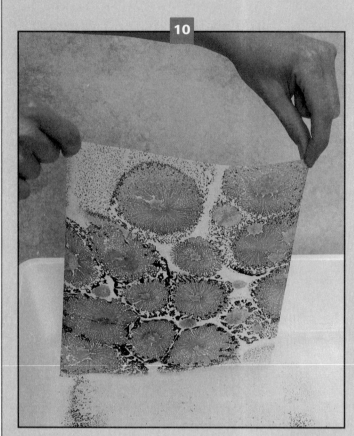

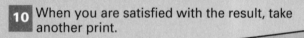

10 When you are satisfied with the result, take another print.

11 More subtle marbling can be achieved by leaving the residue of previous colours in the tray and adding a few drops of white spirit to the surface of the liquid. Agitate the bath with the paint brush to give a softer result, and then take your print.

One of the most fascinating aspects of marbling is that you can experiment endlessly with different colours, and each print you take will be unique.

PAPERCRAFT

HANDMADE BOOK

MATERIALS

To make the handmade book shown *below left* you will need:

Above, cutting board; pencil; ruler; craft knife; two pieces of cardboard, such as mounting card; PVA glue; 20 sheets of A4 paper.

Above: red carpet tape, 5cm wide; 1m length black linen fabric or similar material; 1m red Russian braid; two-hole punch with paper gauge; sail cloth needle or large darning needle; scissors; piece of shiny cloth, such as nylon or silk; old paintbrush.

Books were being made long before the advent of the printing press, and some of the techniques used to make the earliest books still have a purpose today. Here we show you how to make a small notebook, employing one of the simplest and most effective methods of binding loose pages together.

The binding we have used in this lesson (often called Japanese binding) is an ancient technique that originated in the Far East. It involves only the most rudimentary stitching and a minimum of tools: a sharp craft knife, a pot of glue, a darning needle and hole punch are the essential items that you will need.

This method of binding was used in Germany in the period leading up to the First World War by Expressionists such as Erich Heckel and Karl Schmidt-Rottluff, who used it to bind together their dramatic black-and-white woodcut images and text

into starkly beautiful books. In the UK the influence of this binding has been evident in many printed and graphic items since Victorian times, and it is still used for calendars, pattern books, photograph albums and so on.

We have used a dramatic red and black colour scheme for the cover, but you may like to substitute other colours of your own choosing. The carpet tape we have used on the binding — known widely as gaffer tape — is available in a wide choice of colours, and the range of fabric colours is of course almost limitless.

HELPFUL HINT

Shirt boxes or shoe boxes are good sources of card, as they give the correct weight and stiffness for the covers.

P R O J E C T

1 To make the covers, fold a piece of A4 paper into four. Place the paper on a piece of card and use a ruler and pencil to mark out a rectangle about 5mm larger all around than the size of the paper. Cut out the rectangle with the craft knife, using the ruler as a guide. Use the first cover as a template to cut out the second cover.

2 Cut a strip 15mm wide from each piece of card along the lengthwise edge and put the strips to one side. Place one of the covers on the black linen fabric and cut out a piece of fabric approximately 25mm larger all round than the cover. Use this piece of fabric as a template to cut out a second piece.

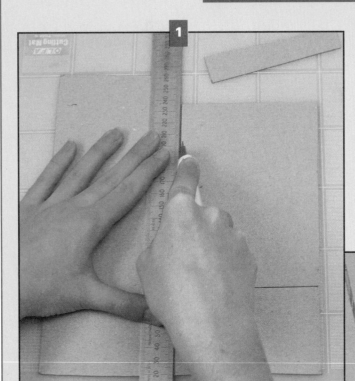

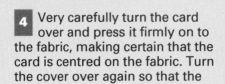

HELPFUL HINT

Keep a jar of water beside you while you are gluing and put the brush in the water immediately after use so that the glue does not harden the bristles.

3 Lay one of the covers in the centre of one of the pieces of fabric. Using a brush, spread the entire surface of one side of the cover with PVA glue, beginning in the centre and working out to the sides. Apply the glue smoothly and evenly with a brush; it should lie like a thin skin on the surface of the card. If there is too much glue it will eventually seep through the fabric.

4 Very carefully turn the card over and press it firmly on to the fabric, making certain that the card is centred on the fabric. Turn the cover over again so that the fabric side is facing you and use a piece of silk or nylon to smooth the fabric and remove any air bubbles. Turn over and press again.

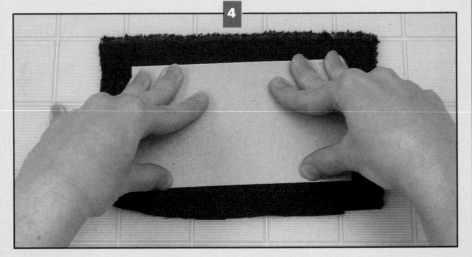

5 Trim the corners of the fabric diagonally as shown, so that each corner of the cardboard almost meets the cutting line but does not protrude over the edge of the fabric.

6 Apply glue around all the edges of the fabric and fold the edges down over the card. Repeat the process from step 3 to cover the other piece of card. Place each cover under a weight and leave until the glue has dried.

7 Cut two strips of red carpet tape, each 25mm longer than the length of the cover. Lay one piece of tape along the lefthand side of one cover — leaving an equal amount of tape free at each end — so that approximately one-third of the width of tape is attached to the cover.

8 Lay one of your narrow strips of card along the centre third of the tape. Cut the corners of the tape diagonally, as you did in step 5 for the corners of the cover fabric.

9 Fold the excess tape at each end over the strip of card.

10 Cut two strips of tape 5 x 2.5cm. Turn the cover over so that the right side is facing you and apply the tape diagonally to the top and bottom uncovered corners. Fold the excess tape around to the wrong side.

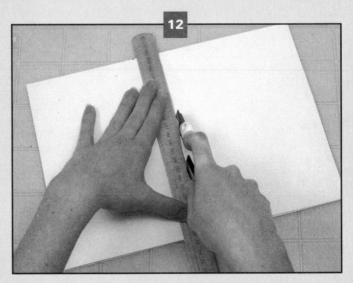

11 To line the inside of the cover, cut a piece of paper to fit and glue it down. Rub the paper gently with the silk or nylon cloth, working into the rough edges of the cover. Repeat the process from step 7 to complete the second cover, applying the long strip of tape to the righthand side and the corner pieces to the opposite corners.

12 To prepare the pages, fold a sheet of A4 paper in half and place it on top of your other A4 sheets. Place a steel ruler on the fold and use the craft knife to cut through all the sheets. (If you have access to a guillotine it will do the job more quickly.)

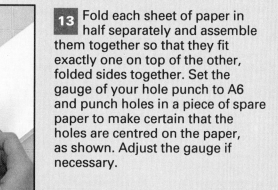

13 Fold each sheet of paper in half separately and assemble them together so that they fit exactly one on top of the other, folded sides together. Set the gauge of your hole punch to A6 and punch holes in a piece of spare paper to make certain that the holes are centred on the paper, as shown. Adjust the gauge if necessary.

14 Punch the paper sheets along their unfolded sides (you may have to do this in several batches if your punch will not easily take them all at once.) Punch a set of holes in both covers, ensuring that when you place the front cover in the punch the outside is facing you, and that when you punch the back cover the outside is facing down.

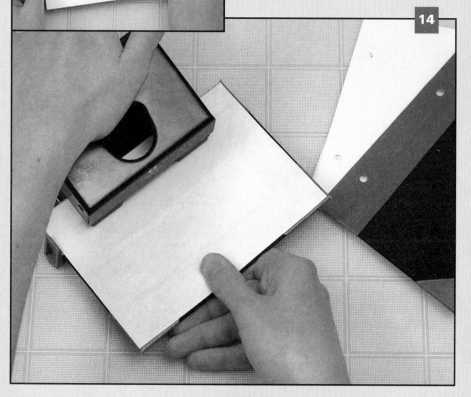

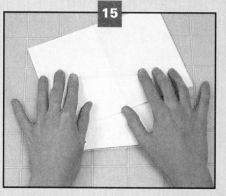

15 Re-assemble the pages and place a piece of blank, spare paper over them so that it covers the edge opposite the holes. Use your finger to rub firmly along the folded edges to flatten them.

16 Place the pages on the edge of your work surface, as shown, and rest the hole punch on top of them so that they remain steady. Cut two strips of tape 5 x 1.25cm, and then cut each one in half to give four strips 2.5 x 1.25cm. Attach two strips at the top of the pile and two strips at the bottom, as shown in the diagram *below*.

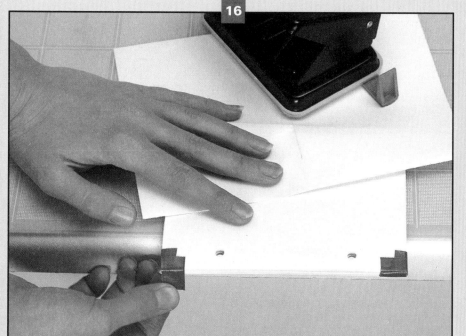

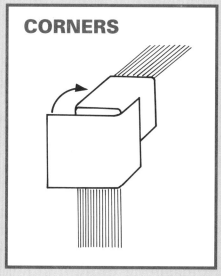

CORNERS

17 Place the pages of the book between the two covers and lay the book on top of a large book, or similar object, so that the edge with the holes is facing you and protruding over the edge of the large book. Make certain that the back of the book is facing downwards. Thread the needle with about 400mm of Russian braid. Put the needle through the top hole, working from the back of the book to the front, and bring the needle to the back (see diagram, *above right*). Insert the needle again from the back to the front and pull up, leaving about 150mm of the end of the braid free. Take the needle and braid around the top of the book and back through the hole (making certain you do not twist the braid), as shown in number 3 of the diagram.

THREADING THE SPINE

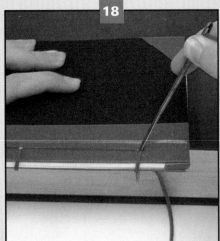

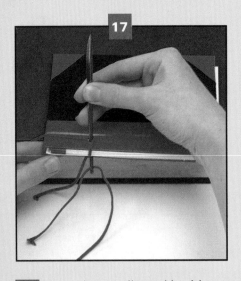

MAKING A POSTAGE KNOT

Make a loop with the lefthand piece of braid and pass the end of the braid through the loop.

Put the righthand piece of braid through the lefthand loop as shown and pull up.

Tie the loose ends together as shown and pull tight.

18 Insert the needle and braid into the bottom hole, from the front to the back. Bring the needle round and insert again, as before. Take the needle around the bottom of the book; making certain that the braid is not twisted, and insert into the hole again from the top, as shown.

19 Turn the book over so that the front is face down and tie the ends of the braid in a postage knot (see Making a Postage Knot, *left*).

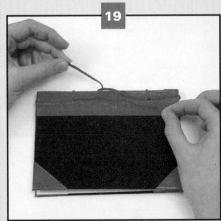

You can use this design and binding to make other useful books such as an address book, diary or sketchbook, or even a book of your own poems or drawings. You can also decorate the front cover with a simple motif or lettering, as we have done (see page 93). Simply draw your design on a piece of paper or card and glue it in place.

PRINTMAKING

LINOCUT BOOKPLATE

MATERIALS

To print the bookplates shown *left* you will need:

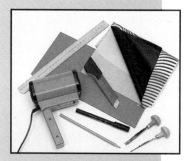

Above: block of lino, at least 110 x 155mm; hairdryer; tracing paper; carbon paper; HB pencil; craft knife and metal ruler; waterproof felt-tip pen; V-shaped tool and U-shaped gouge.

Above: a rubber roller at least 110mm wide; sheet of glass or plastic, melamine or other non-porous surface to roll the ink on; 32ml tube of oil-based printing ink in black; an old palette knife; sheets of Japanese paper (or thin cartridge paper) for printing on (each sheet should be at least 120 x 160mm); wooden spoon; rags and white spirit; Blu-Tack; acid-free paper adhesive.

A linocut is one of the simplest forms of printmaking, and this attractive bookplate, which uses only one colour, is a practical introduction to the art. You can ring the changes by printing on coloured paper to tone or contrast with the endpapers of your books.

Linocutting is a relief printing process — the artist begins with a flat surface and cuts into it to give a block with raised areas and lower areas. Ink is then applied to the surface with a roller, covering the raised areas only. This means that, when you print, the areas cut away remain white and the raised, inked surfaces print the design. The print is taken by placing a piece of paper on the inked surface of the block and burnishing it (rubbing it) so that the ink is transferred to the paper. Although it is possible to design linocuts composed of several colours, our bookplate is in black only. A richly decorative effect is obtained by printing it on coloured Japanese paper.

Linoleum is made of a mixture of linseed oil, powdered cork, chalk, resin and pigment (if it is coloured) on a woven jute backing. It is available in various thicknesses, but for the purpose of making a linocut, it should be at least 3mm thick. Artist's quality lino is available from specialist suppliers, or you can use ordinary flooring lino provided the surface is flat, unpatterned and not too hard. Do not use old lino, as it becomes brittle as the linseed oil dries out.

Special inks are available for printing linocuts. Choose between oil- and water-based inks, bearing in mind that oil-based inks are more permanent but may be messier to work with, and tools must be cleaned with white spirit.

Choosing paper

You can use almost any absorbent paper for linocuts. The thinner the paper, however, the less absorbent it will be. Thin paper will require less burnishing to achieve an even print. It is a good idea to choose thin paper for bookplates, so that the paper does not put any strain on the endpaper.

Above: A selection of Japanese handmade papers.

LINOCUTTING BLADES

It is worth using good quality tools which can be re-sharpened, with handles which fit comfortably in your hand.

If you want to experiment with a variety of blades, you can buy a handle with interchangeable blades, but these will become blunt after you have cut a couple of blocks.

For this project, only two blades are used; a narrow V-shaped tool, for cutting the outlines and details, and a wider U-shaped gouge for clearing the areas to be left white.

MAKING THE JIG

A jig makes cutting the lino block easier, as it stops the lino from moving as you cut into it. We show you below how to make a simple jig.

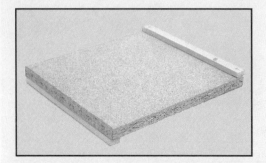

Above: Apply glue down the length of one strip of wood and position it along one edge of the piece of chipboard. Nail in place. Turn the wood over, and glue and nail the other strip of

MATERIALS

To make a simple jig you will need a piece of chipboard, 25cm square; two 10 x 18mm wooden strips, each 25cm long; wood glue; 2cm nails; hammer.

wood along the opposite edge as shown. When using the jig, position it so that the strip of wood underneath fits over one edge of the work surface.

USING THE TOOLS

Before starting the project, practise using the tools. Try cutting a curve, a circle and a straight line with each tool. Grip the handle in the palm of your hand and push it along the lines of the design, always working away from you. Practise stopping the cut at an exact point, then lifting the tool and turning it to change direction. Do not cut too deep, or the tool will get stuck.

The U-shaped gouge, *right*, cuts a wide area. The deeper you cut, the larger the white area.

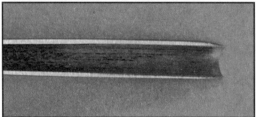
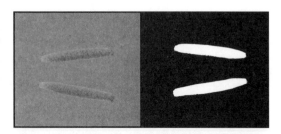

The V-shaped tool, *right*, can be used to cut very fine lines. Again, the deeper you cut into the surface, the wider the white area will be.

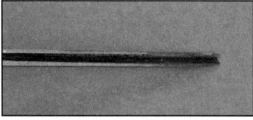
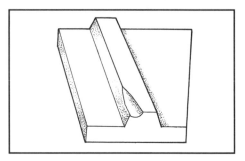

Avoid undercutting the surface of the lino as this will trap ink during the printing process. Undercut edges are easily damaged.

When cutting away lino to leave narrow strips, use the V-shaped tool to cut sloping sides which support the surface of the lino.

Avoid damaging the cut edges of the block. You should always ensure that the blades you use are kept sharp.

PROJECT

THE DESIGN

1 Trace the design, *above* (or photocopy it). Place carbon paper over the block, carbon side down, and put the tracing on top. Go over the design in pencil, pressing firmly.

2 Remove the paper and carbon, then go over the outline on the block with a waterproof felt-tip pen.

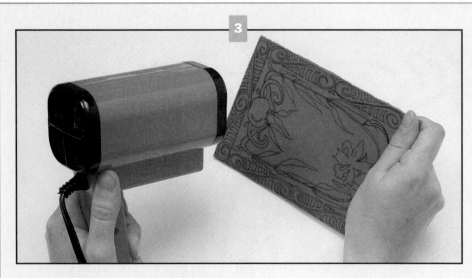

3 In order to make the block easier to work with, warm it using a hairdryer. Or use a damp towel and an iron, or hot water bottle, or warm it on a radiator. Repeat this if the block hardens as you are working on it.

4 Before you start cutting out the design, you may find it helpful to fill in the areas to be retained with felt-tip pen. Put the block in the jig and cut around the outlines of the design, using the V-shaped tool. Keep the lines fluid, cutting out only the area to be left white.

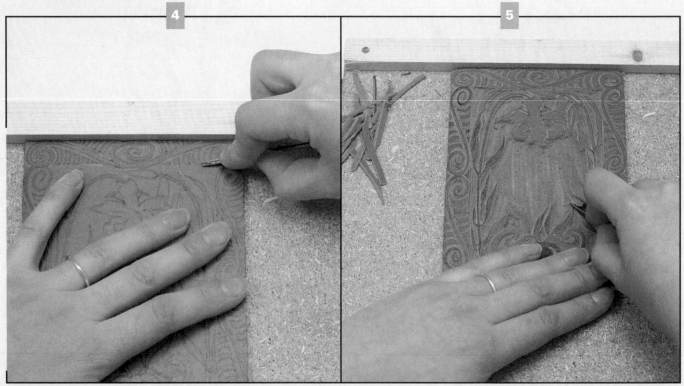

5 Use the U-shaped gouge to remove the larger areas of white. When you have finished cutting, turn the block upside down and tap it so that all the loose bits of lino fall out.

6 Stick the sheet of glass down on the work surface using blobs of Blu-Tack, or tape down the edges with parcel tape. Squeeze about a teaspoon of black, oil-based ink on to the glass inking surface. Spread it out thinly with the palette knife. Then use the roller to spread the ink across the glass, ensuring that the roller is evenly covered (*below*).

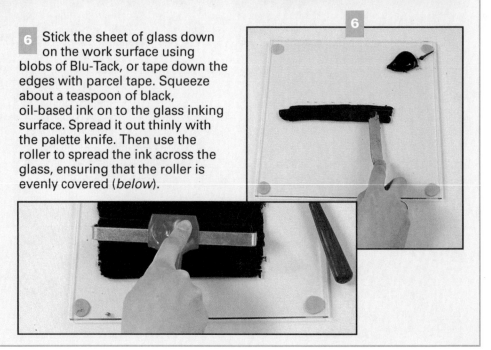

7 Roll the inked roller over the lino block, getting as much ink on to the raised surfaces as possible without getting ink into the cut out parts. Re-charge the roller with ink when necessary. (If the block does get over-inked, you can clean it off with white spirit and start again.)

8 Hold the paper horizontally above the block, and lower it straight down on to it.

9 Press the paper down with the palm of the hand so that it sticks to the block.

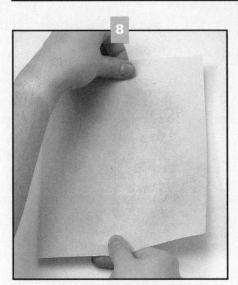

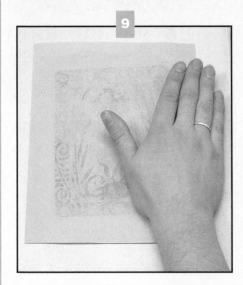

10 To make the print, burnish over the paper lightly using the back of a wooden spoon, rubbing in a circular motion.

Burnish evenly over the entire surface of the block, making sure the paper doesn't shift. The design will show through the paper.

11 Lift one corner of the paper to see if the design has printed and continue to burnish if necessary. You will find that the first print may be a little speckled — this is because the lino absorbs some of the ink to start with. Later printings will be more solid.

12 When a satisfactory print has been made, peel the paper carefully off the block and leave to dry. Continue to print as many bookplates as you want, adding more ink to the glass plate as necessary (one teaspoon of ink is enough for three prints).

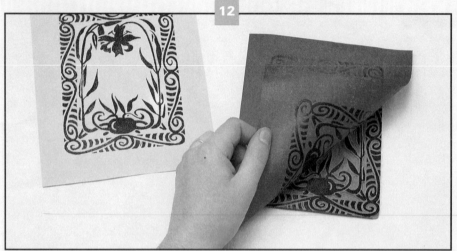

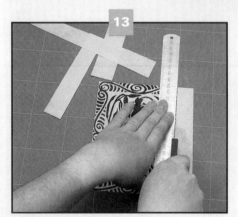

13 The prints will take at least 24 hours to dry completely. When they are dry, trim the bookplates to size, using a craft knife and a metal straight edge. To use your bookplate, first write your name in the central area. Then stick the bookplate on the front endpaper of a book, using paper adhesive.

Cleaning

To clean the block and roller, wipe with newspaper, then clean thoroughly using a rag dampened with white spirit. To clean the inking surface, first scrape off any surplus ink with the palette knife, and wipe with newspaper. Then clean thoroughly using a rag and white spirit.

PAPERCRAFT

BOOKBINDING

MATERIALS

To re-bind the book shown *below left* you will need:

Above, paperback book, 182 x 259mm; 30 x 40cm sheet of 2mm greyboard; 30 x 30cm piece of bookbinding cloth; A2 sheet of cartridge paper for endpapers; cutting mat; 6 x 30cm strip of jaconet (bookbinding linen); metal rule; straight edge; PVA glue; newsprint; craft knife; bone folder; 5cm decorator's brush; jam jar.

Above, A4 sheet of marbled paper (see page 89); 2 wooden boards 20 x 30cm; sheet of white transfer lettering; pencil; small brush; heavy weight.

Bookbinding is a useful and venerable craft, and in this project we show you how to make a suitable showcase for your calligraphic skills by turning an old paperback into an attractively bound book.

A professional bookbinder's work involves not only creating new objects, such as the handmade book and bookplate that we have already made, but also the conservation and restoration of damaged books. In this project we have re-bound a paperback exhibition catalogue with a hard cover to give it a longer life, but you could also bind a plain paper notebook to contain your calligraphy in the same way.

The pages of the book we have re-bound were folded and sewn together in sections. Many paperbacks, however, are 'perfect bound', with individual pages glued together at the spine. This type of binding is generally more prone to wear and tear; with time the glue loses its flexibility and pages may fall out. Look at the top of the spine of your book to determine the type of binding — if it is perfect bound you may need to strengthen the spine by following the Helpful Hint on page 106.

We have given instructions for estimating the quantities of materials you will need on page 106. The book we re-bound has a page size of 182 x 259mm. If your book is smaller than this you may wish to use narrower strips of bookcloth to give more suitable proportions to the area of cover paper in relation to the size of the book.

PARTS OF A BOOK

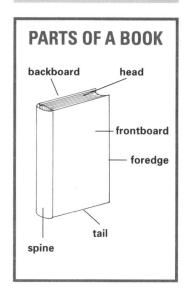

PROJECT

ESTIMATING MATERIALS

If you are re-binding a book a different size from ours, you will need to estimate the quantity of materials required. First measure your book and write down the length and width of the page and the spine. Then use the instructions and diagram below as a guide to actual quantities of materials you will need. Remember to buy more than you need to allow for the fact that the grain of the paper should run along the length of the book. It is important to cut the materials as you work rather than preparing them beforehand.

Cartridge paper endpapers: two pieces of paper, each twice the size of the page of the book. Each endpaper is folded in half (see step 2).

Jaconet: a strip the width of the spine of the book plus an extra 40mm, and 10mm shorter than the spine in length.

Greyboard: a front and back cover board, a piece for the spine and the spine template (see diagram).

Bookcloth: one spine piece and two edge strips (see diagram, dotted lines).

Marbled cover paper: two pieces the same length as the boards, plus an extra 40mm; the same width as the part of the board not covered by the bookcloth, plus an additional 6mm.

Wooden pressing boards: these should be slightly larger than the book.

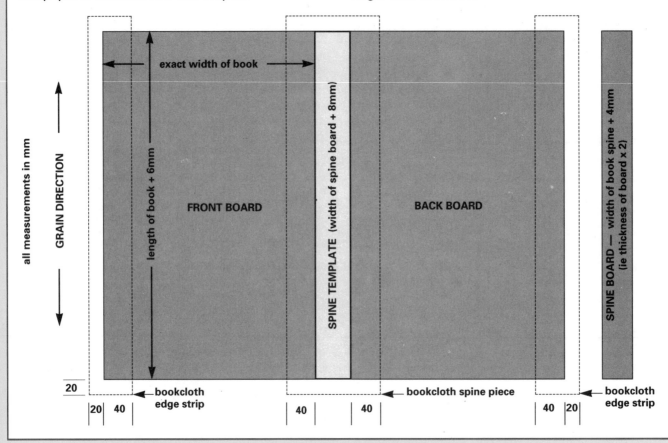

all measurements in mm

GRAIN DIRECTION

exact width of book

length of book + 6mm

FRONT BOARD

SPINE TEMPLATE (width of spine board + 8mm)

BACK BOARD

SPINE BOARD — width of book spine + 4mm (ie thickness of board x 2)

20

← bookcloth edge strip

← bookcloth spine piece

← bookcloth edge strip

20 | 40

40 | 40

40 | 20

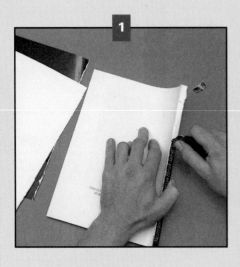

1 | Carefully tear the front and back covers from the book and peel the cover from the spine with your fingers and a craft knife, making sure that you do not tear the pages or remove the glue.

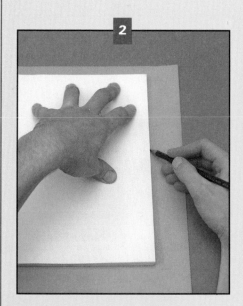

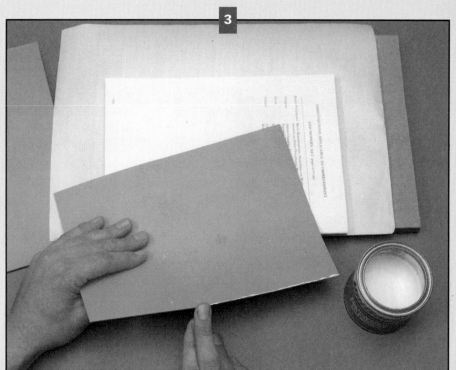

2 Check the direction of the grain of the cartridge paper for the endpapers by wetting one corner. The grain runs along the slight curl that will result. Fold the paper in half along the grain, and align the spine of the book with the fold. Draw around three sides of the book with a pencil. Remove the book and cut the endpaper with a knife and straight edge. Repeat for the other endpaper.

3 Put a piece of newsprint on a wooden board and place the book on the board with the spine slightly overhanging it. With your finger, dab PVA glue on to the top of the folded edge of one of the endpapers, as shown. Turn the endpaper over and glue flush with the spine. Rub down firmly. Turn the book over and repeat on the other side. Put a wooden board on top. Leave to dry for 10 minutes.

4 Cut a strip of jaconet for the spine (see Estimating materials box). Place a piece of newsprint on a wooden board and brush PVA glue on to the spine, rubbing the glue well into the spine to strengthen it. (You do not need to glue in this way if you have had to repair the spine, see Helpful Hint, page 106.) Leave to dry.

5 Brush a second coat of PVA glue on to the spine. Centre the strip of jaconet on the spine (with a 20mm overlap on both sides) and rub with your finger. Use the bone folder to smooth the spine down evenly. The jaconet adds more strength to the spine.

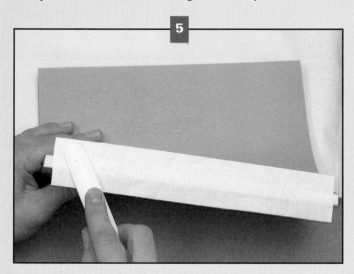

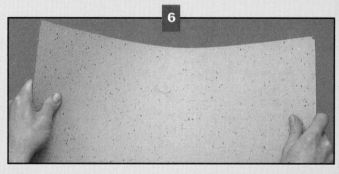

6 Bend the greyboard to find the grain direction. The edge that bends more easily has the grain running from top to bottom. Mark with an arrow.

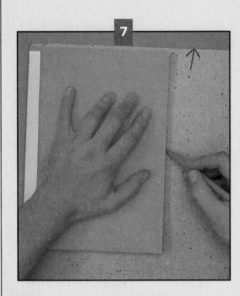

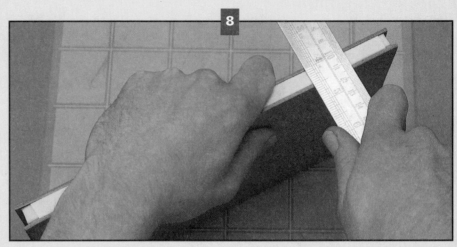

7 Line up the spine of the book with the edge of the board along the grain, 6mm from the top of the board. With a pencil, draw around the foredge and the tail of the book. Mark out a second board in the same way. Cut both boards with a knife and straight edge.

8 To measure the width of the spine board, place the book inside the front and back boards and take a measurement from the outside of one edge to the outside of the other edge. The length of the spine is the same as the front and back boards. Cut out a piece of greyboard to these measurements. Now cut a template for the spine: this is a piece of greyboard the same length as the spine board and 8mm wider. (The template is used to space the bookcloth at the spine to allow the book to open and close freely.)

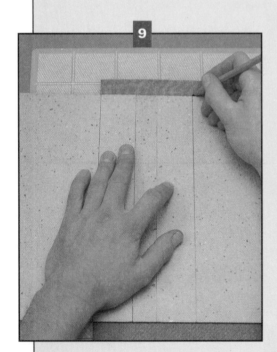

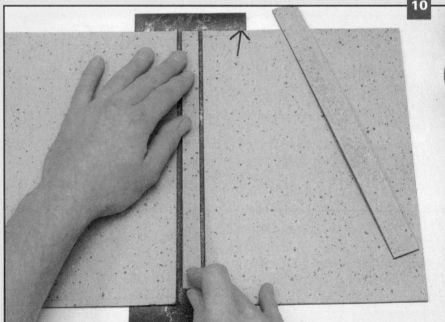

9 Draw pencil lines 40mm from the foredge and spine edge of the front and back boards. Put the spine template on the bookcloth between the boards and mark the width of the bookcloth for the spine. Measure and mark the strips of bookcloth for the outer edges of the boards (see page 106). Cut out the pieces of bookcloth with a knife and straight edge.

10 Lay the bookcloth spine piece on a sheet of newsprint and stipple the spine with PVA glue using the decorator's brush. Discard the newsprint you have just used and replace it with a fresh sheet. Put one of the cover boards on the table and place the bookcloth spine (glue side down) on top of it, lining up one bookcloth edge with the 40mm pencil line on the board (leaving a 20mm overlap at top and bottom). Press gently with your hand and then turn the board and cloth over. Place the spine template on the bookcloth next to the board, then place the other cover board accurately in position. Turn the assembled boards over and rub with your hand. Turn the boards over again and remove the template. Stipple more PVA glue on to the cloth and place the spine board centrally between the cover boards (with a 4mm gap on both sides) as shown. Press the spine down firmly. Stipple a little more PVA glue on the bookcloth overlaps if necessary, then turn them over and rub down.

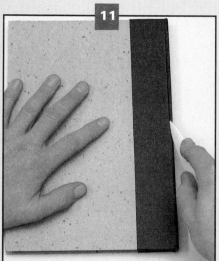

11 Place the book inside the covers, flush with the spine, and close the covers. Press the end of the bone folder gently into the crease between the cover boards and spine board to create a sharp fold. Mark the front of one endpaper and the inside of the corresponding front board with a cross to ensure that you assemble the covers on the book in the same way that you creased the folds of the spine. Remove the book.

12 Apply glue to a bookcloth edge strip, line it up with the pencil line on one of the boards and glue in position. Turn the boards over, cut the corners of the bookcloth at a 45º angle, 2mm from the board, rub down the head and tail turnovers, push the corner in with the bone folder and carefully rub down the long turnover. Repeat the procedure for the other board.

HELPFUL HINT

Before assembling the book in its covers you may wish to add lettering to the spine of the book. This can be done with transfer lettering. Draw a pencil line for the bottom of the type and rub down the letters with a pencil, spacing them carefully. If you make any mistakes, lift the letters off with masking tape. To fix the letters, with a small brush apply a thin layer of watered-down PVA glue, which will act as a transparent varnish.

13 Measure 5mm from the edge of the boards on the turnovers of the bookcloth and trim all round with a knife and steel rule.

14 Cut out the marbled cover papers (see Estimating materials box). Dilute the PVA glue with a little water, and stipple on to the back of the paper. Glue in position on the outside of the boards with a 3mm overlap on the bookcloth and a 20mm turnover at head and tail. Rub down the turnovers on the inside and trim.

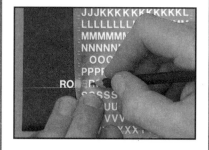

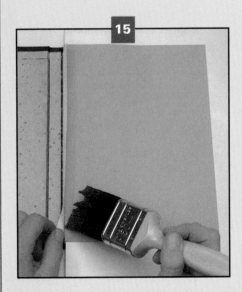

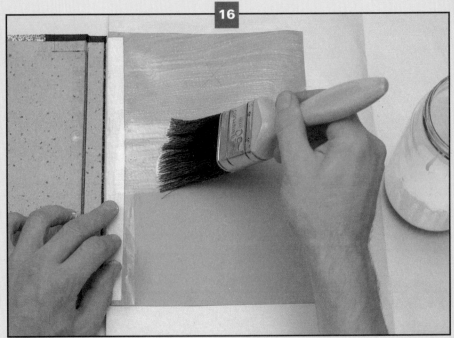

15 Place the book inside the cover, matching up the crosses on the board and the endpaper, and lining up the edge of the spine of the book with the edge of the back board. Make sure that the boards have an even 3mm overlap at the head, tail and foredge. Place a sheet of newsprint between the front endpapers. Stipple a little watered-down PVA glue between the jaconet flap and the endpaper and rub down.

16 Working quickly, glue the endpaper, working from the spine to the foredge. Remove the newsprint and close the board down on the book. Glue the jaconet and endpaper to the other side of the book in the same way. Open the book to check that the endpapers are stuck down and smooth them with your hand if necessary.

17 Cover a board with a sheet of newsprint and place the book on the board with the spine protruding slightly. Place a sheet of newsprint and the second board on top of the book. Place a weight on the board and press for a minute. Open the book to check that the endpapers are glued evenly. Replace the book in the boards under a weight for 48 hours. Any small air bubbles will disappear when the glue has dried.

Choose a cover paper to reflect the subject of your book, and make sure that your endpapers match the cover. You could also use marbled paper for the endpapers of the book.

Incipit officii beate Marie virginis
secundum consuetudinem Romane cu
rie. Ad matutinum. vers.
Domine labia mea aperies
Et os meum annunciabit la
udem tuam. V. Deus in adiutorium
meum intende. R. Domine ad adiuuan
dum me festina. Gloria patri et filio. Sic
inuit. Aue Maria gratia plena. Dominus tecum
Enite exultemus domino in